Moments on the Mount

Moments on the Mount

Ralph Sweet

SWEET PUBLISHING COMPANY
Austin   Texas 78765

PRINTED IN U.S.A.

STANDARD BOOK NUMBER: 8344-0047-2

PREFACE

This abridged study of the Sermon on the Mount is an attempt to delve into the depths of the teachings of Jesus. The author believes that Jesus gives the key to many perplexing problems if we will but "find" the answer.

Many of the basic ideas come from *The Psychology of Christian Personality* by Ernest Ligon. This book, although written many years ago, has been a source of great inspiration not only for some of these lessons, but also for daily living.

These lessons have been given to audiences in various places. The reaction has been the same; people are hungry for the real truth of the teachings of Jesus. After all, did he not say, "ye shall know the truth and the truth shall make you free"? Searching and delving into his words will make us free—free from sin, worry, pessimism, unhappiness, and above all, free from ourselves.

CONTENTS

Chapter 1

Introduction

DO YOU RECALL the story of Aladdin and his magic lamp? Children are fascinated by the account of how Aladdin's wonderful lamp procured for him anything his heart desired. Today there is no geni on the loose as there was in Aladdin's day, but the twentieth century has witnessed wonders about which Aladdin never dreamed. There is no "magic" here, however, for men of science have accomplished their feats by understanding and controlling the forces of nature.

Because of the triumph of science, many individuals no longer have any use for religion; science and religion are generally thought to be miles apart. But there are similarities between science and religion that are often overlooked and even denied by some scientists.

Science and Religion

In the first place, scientists assume that the universe is orderly. If the universe were not orderly it would be impossible to make predictions, for one would not know what was going to happen next. Yet, the motions of the planets are so orderly that astronomers can predict an eclipse of the sun to a fraction of a second.

Does this not imply something for religion? Does it not imply that the God who governs the universe through physical laws governs the spiritual world by laws just as certain and just as unchangeable as the law of gravitation and the laws of planetary motion? If the teachings of Jesus are correct, faith and love are spiritual forces as great as any ever found in the natural sciences. Man cannot change the truth of the laws of nature, yet many individuals think they can tamper with God's spiritual laws. Simply denying the law of gravity does not make it invalid. In a similar way, a person can deny the doctrine of heaven and hell; yet the force of the laws of faith and love will be unchanged.

A second assumption of science is that the true explanation is the one which best fits the facts. No scientist ever saw an atom, yet he assumes that atoms exist in order to explain the scientific phenomena he examines in his laboratory. Without the atomic hypothesis, he could not exploit the forces of nature in the way that he does.

The same principle holds true in religion. Theologians of the past have offered "proofs" for the existence of God, but these were not proofs that appealed to the five senses. A close examination of the logical arguments for the existence of God will reveal that most of them implicitly assume that to believe in God is the best way to explain such things as the existence of the universe, the design of the world, man's moral sense, or even our idea of God itself.

Another assumption of science is that a small sampling of a phenomenon reveals truth about the rest of the force which is being measured. There is no way of checking every possible case in which the law of gravity is involved; but science, by investigating selected instances, discovers truth about nature in general. This likewise has an application in religion. One's attitudes generally display his spiritual condition. This is not to say that attitudes comprise the whole of spiritual life, but the healthiness of one's attitudes will probably indicate whether or not he is living in conformity to the spiritual laws of the universe. If God is good, as the Bible reveals him to be, surely mental health will be one of the rewards of obeying his spiritual laws. It is hard to believe that God would so order the universe that godliness produces unhappiness and mental disorder.

Jesus insisted that happiness is a part of the Christian life. Yet there are Christians who are terribly unhappy—who are sour on the world and who have not found the peace that passes understanding. Does this mean that Christianity has failed? Or does it only mean that the transforming power of the teachings of Jesus have been overlooked in the life of this individual? Surely it must be the latter.

Misguided Religious Education

Part of the blame for wrong attitudes may lie in misguided programs of religious education. It is wrong to assume that all education that is religious is healthy. An example of misguided religious education is the "thou shalt not" type of education. Many individuals believe that the chief function of religion is to tell one what he must not do, and that the chief motivation for this is shame. To discover that this was not the teaching of Jesus one has only to study the Sermon on the Mount. In contrast to the negative morality of the scribes and Pharisees, Jesus taught a positive approach to life that produces happiness and abundant living.

A second kind of misguided religious education is that which seeks to instill religious facts. This theory of education is based on the assumption that knowledge of the historical and geographical facts of the Bible will automatically produce moral and religious behavior. Yet there is no evidence that this is the case.

A third type of educational activity is the "rally-day" method which aims at large numbers and big programs. The chief motivation here is usually loyalty to the church and fear of displeasing those in authority. This is not to say that numbers are unimportant, for every number represents a soul. The point is that a religious education program based solely on an appeal for huge crowds is unhealthy.

A fourth type of religious education is that which totally misses the demands of practical living. Men are not helped by high-sounding phrases and flowery descriptions. Few are helped by sermons or lessons based on abstract generalities or polished rhetoric.

An important fact to remember in planning Bible school programs is that men come to the study of the Bible with different abilities and capacities and will therefore respond in different ways. Jesus taught this great truth in the parable of the sower (Matt. 13:1-9). There will always be the thirtyfold, sixtyfold and one-hundredfold Christian.

Each individual develops in his own way because he is endowed with different abilities and capacities. As a child begins to learn to live in the world around him, he quickly discovers that his natural abilities and appetites must be modified in certain ways. A person's education is really an effort to discover how his appetites and urges and abilities can be satisfied. A person generally adopts those habits which furnish satisfaction for him. As a child matures he will develop his system of values, likes and dislikes, fears, angers and loves. If, in his social activity, an urge finds no immediate satisfaction, an emotion arises.

For example, if a person is hungry and he believes that no food will be available, he is likely to become afraid. Or if he discovers that food is available but someone is withholding it from him, he will become angry. Finally, if someone satisfies these urges, his emotion will be love. The sum total of these reactions to the world are generally called one's emotional attitudes. The kind of personality and the health of mind of the individual depends upon the emotional attitudes that he develops.

It goes without saying that not all emotional attitudes are healthy. Some emotional attitudes are decidedly unhealthy; others are completely wholesome. The important thing to remember is that these emotional attitudes are not inherited. Each person develops and learns them as a result of experience. Regardless of one's present emotional attitudes, he can change them. Why should they be changed? Because some attitudes produce nothing but unhappiness—to say nothing of their being out of harmony with God's revealed will.

Sources of Harmony and Conflict

The human body is a mechanism which, like all mechanisms, can operate either harmoniously or unharmoniously. The mind, in a similar way, can operate either harmoniously or it can be in inner conflict. Lack of harmony in mental attitudes may be harder to detect, although one can discover from the mentally ill the extreme attitudes that constitute mental illness. A rough and simplified classification places personalities into three groups according to the extend and nature of their inner harmony or conflict.

The so-called psychopathic personality is the first group. This person tries to satisfy each instinctive urge whenever it appears in the most primitive fashion. This rule of life is "I want what I want, when I want it." His personality is dominated by the emotion of the moment. He had no purpose in life and his desire for achievement is never satisfied. This results in unhappiness.

At the other extreme is the inhibited personality. Often, a child who has only been taught a negative morality of "thou shalt not" begins to feel that all his urges and appetites are sinful. He becomes ashamed of them and refuses to admit them even to himself. Although a person such as this has banished these urges from his conscious mind, he cannot banish them from his personality. They will express themselves in one form or another, often making the individual frustrated and unhappy.

Finally, there is the individual who succeeds in forming a harmony of healthy attitudes so that all his energy is directed to one common purpose. A dominant purpose in life is essential to a healthy attitude. This can be seen among college students. Those who do the best work are the ones who have a goal and know where they are going.

An increasing number of men who are investigating the workings of the human mind have discovered that to be happy, one's central purpose in life must be directed toward others. The man whose only purpose in life is himself will never find happiness. This is significant in light of the teachings of Jesus. Not only must one have a dominant purpose in life, this purpose must be in line with one's abilities. An individual must not attempt something for which he has no ability; yet he must find a purpose which makes use of all his abilities. One must have faith in his ability, faith in the value of his work and faith in the importance of society. These are attitudes that Jesus emphasized in his teaching.

The healthy and harmonious personality can be destroyed by the wrong attitudes. If an individual allows unbridled appetites and urges to dominate his life, his mental condition will be one of extreme unhappiness. If the psychologist were to name the two principle causes of unhappiness he would probably name fear and anger. These two emotions are at the very base of most of our unhappiness. A happy personality cannot tolerate these conditions. It is significant that Jesus said so much about both of them.

Faith and Love

Jesus, the son of the Living God, understood people better than anyone who ever lived. His teachings are admired and respected even by those who reject his divinity. Unfortunately, men too often read his teachings like the verses of some beautiful poem—they consider them challenging and lofty, but impractical and too idealistic. Others interpret them superficially and quite often miss their deeper meanings.

Consider Jesus' demand for faith. Almost every religion emphasizes faith, but Jesus gave a new and precise meaning to it. For him faith was not merely mental assent. The faith he demanded is not to be like the faith by which the facts of history are ac-cepted. Neither is faith to be the blind superstition of the ignorant nor the pious belief of the uncritical. Both of these types of faith have had their influence—but these are not the faith taught by Jesus. Jesus demanded faith in his teachings because they were necessary for abundant living. He did not urge obedience only because of his own authority. Indeed, one of the things which astonished his hearers was that he did not appeal to older authorities as the scribes and Pharisees did, but appealed instead to universal experience. The authority of the teachings of Jesus is based on the fact that they will bring happiness and joy in living. Notice in particular the ethical demands of the Sermon on the Mount. "Love your enemies and pray for those who persecute you." "Judge not, that you be not judged." "Seek first his kingdom and his righteousness, and all these things shall be yours as well." Jesus did not demand these things only because of duty nor because they are right or wrong. His appeal was based on the fact that these things will bring happiness and the abundant life both now and in the hereafter.

Jesus also taught that love is a great source of spiritual strength. Yet love, like faith, is often misunderstood. Love can mean many things, and in the Greek language there are several different words that are all translated as the English word "love." The phrase "Christian love" is often used in an effort to capture what Jesus meant, but this is just a way of avoiding the difficulty. The term "brotherly love" has also been used to try to describe what Jesus meant, but just what brotherly love means is not commonly agreed upon. A misunderstanding of what Jesus meant by love results in a misunderstanding of his commandments. Loving one's enemies has been looked upon by some as impossible. Others think that turning the other cheek is an act of cowardice. To return good for evil and to pray for those who are wicked is too hard for most. Even brotherly love seems inadequate to explain what Jesus had in mind.

Fatherly Love

It is only when one realizes that Jesus taught fatherly love, not brotherly love, that these teachings come into focus. Christians are to have a love that transcends brotherly affection. They are to love others as a father loves his son. Notice what a change this makes in the application of the commands of Jesus. "Love your enemies" has been a difficult commandment. But no one thinks David was abnormal because he loved Absalom even when he was in open rebellion. What father does not turn his cheek to his son hundreds of times? What parent would fail to pray for a child who was even at that moment despitefully using him? How frequently parents bless their children when the children in return curse them. Fathers constantly return good for evil and love their children even when they are unlovable.

14

Introduction

Fatherly love destroys fear and anger. Anger is not the characteristic response of parents to children and parents lose all fear for their own safety out of love for their children. A mother will rush into a burning building in an effort to save a sleeping child, with no thought of safety for herself. There is no attitude that Christians could have toward others that would be any more healthful, from a psychological point of view, than the fatherly love Jesus taught in the Sermon on the Mount.

This does not mean that Christians are to go around being "fatherly" to everyone in the ordinary sense of the term. What this does mean is that Christians are to study the teachings of Jesus, with particular reference to that collection of teachings known as the Sermon on the Mount, to discover proper attitudes toward others. We will discover that we are to love others with the same love that our Father in heaven has for us, so that we may be "perfect, as your heavenly Father is perfect."

Questions

1. What are the similarities between science and religion? What assumptions does each make that are similar?
2. What kind of evidence do "proofs" for God's existence offer? What assumption is at the basis of these logical arguments? How is Hebrews 11:6 relevant to a discussion of proofs for the existence of God?
3. Discuss the various kinds of misguided religious education. How is the wrong kind of education responsible for unhealthy attitudes?
4. How does the parable of the sower relate itself to a discussion of religious education? What provisions should be made in an educational program for various abilities?
5. How does a person obtain his emotional attitudes? Are they inherited? Can he do anything to change then? Should he want to change them?
6. What are some examples of a psychopathic personality? Would an uncontrollable temper be an example of an "I-want-what-I-want-when-I-want-it" attitude?
7. What attitudes will an exclusively negative religious education program produce? What is meant by repression?
8. What are some of the characteristics of a healthy personality? How are these things reflected in the teachings of Jesus?

9. How can a healthy personality be destroyed by the wrong kind of attitudes? What are some of these attitudes?
10. What kind of faith did Jesus demand of his followers? Did Jesus appeal only to his authority as the son of God? Is there any practical reason for accepting the commands of Jesus?
11. How does the love commanded by Jesus differ from what is usually denoted by the term "brotherly love?" Discuss how fatherly love clarifies the ethical demands of Jesus.

Chapter 2

The Key to Happiness

THE FIRST WORD in the Sermon on the Mount is "happy." This Greek word is usually translated into English as "blessed," although it can also mean "happy," as it does in 1 Corinthians 7:40.

If the word "happy" is read in place of "blessed" in these eight beatitudes, one can see that Jesus is stating a set of powerful principles which will bring happiness and peace of mind to the individual who follows them. These beatitudes are not to be understood as a set of moral principles or ethical commands, but as a statement of fact. The one who develops these attitudes in his life will find abundant living in the kingdom of God.

The Quest

Men have sought for happiness in a variety of ways, all of which have one thing in common—they seek to satisfy man's needs and appetites. These are really two ways to go about finding happiness. The first way is to attempt to develop an environment which will satisfy one's every wish. This is often the road to happiness the wealthy pursue. The second way of finding happiness is to develop those personality traits that will enable an individual to be happy in any environment.

Jesus taught that the way to lasting happiness is in the development of right attitudes. This truth is echoed throughout his teachings and is summed up in the eight principles usually called the beatitudes. If a man can develop these attitudes of heart, he will be happy in wealth or in poverty. For the purposes of this discussion, these eight principles will be considered in slightly different order than they are presented in the fifth chapter of Matthew. This lesson will deal with the four principles of faith. The next lesson will consider the four principles of fatherly love.

The Poor in Spirit

Happy are the poor in spirit: for theirs is the kingdom of heaven.
Matthew 5:3

The audience to whom Jesus spoke shared the popular misconception that wealth is the road to happiness. Poverty seemed to them to be the foundation of the world's misery. Although poverty of material goods and poverty of the spirit are not the same thing, they are closely related. An individual who is wealthy in material goods is likely to feel self-sufficient and self-satisfied. A good example of this is the parable of the rich farmer who resolved in his heart to tear down his old barns and build better and bigger ones to hold the bounty of his harvest (Luke 12:16-21). This rich farmer needed help from no one. He was completely self sufficient, and in turn was smug and self-assured. He had none of the poverty of spirit that Jesus stressed was so important.

A man who is poor in spirit realizes his insufficiency. He acknowledges that he has much to learn and that there are greater things to be accomplished in the future. He is dissatisfied with his present accomplishments and looks forward to the greater victories that lie ahead.

A striking illustration of the difference between wealth of spirit and poverty of spirit is found in the parable of the Pharisee and the publican. The Pharisee, in his own mind, was spiritually rich. He needed nothing because, in his opinion, he was perfect. The parable describes him as praying to himself, not to God. He bragged about how righteous he was, and thanked God that he was wealthy in spiritual values. The publican, on the other hand, had no doubt about his own spiritual poverty. His prayer was heard because he acknowledged his own inadequacy.

A man who is rich in spirit is generally an individual who thinks he knows it all. It is difficult to get him to study the Bible because he feels no real need for it. This individual tends to be dogmatic and confident in his own judgment and infallibility. He becomes proud and haughty. He is typified by all that is implied in the term "Pharisaic."

This individual will not be happy since one of his basic needs is thwarted by his attitude. One of the greatest sources of happiness is a sense of achievement. The rich in spirit are seldom ambitious for achievement for they are satisfied with things as they are. There is no room for improvement as far as they are concerned, and their personalities become stagnant.

The poor in spirit, on the other hand, have a vision of higher things. They are never complacent and self-satisfied. Their attitude stimulates achievement, which is a basic source of happiness. The one who is poor in spirit is ever learning and ever yearning for better things. The Apostle Paul exemplified this spiritual poverty when he wrote: "Not that I have already obtained this or am already perfect; but I press on to make it my own, because Christ Jesus has made me his own. Brethren, I do not consider that I have made it my own; but one thing I do, forgetting what lies behind and straining forward to what lies ahead, I press on toward the goal for the prize of the upward call of God in Christ Jesus" (Philippians 3:12-16). It is significant that the key word in the Philippian letter is "rejoice."

Spiritual Hunger

Happy are they who hunger and thirst after righteousness: for they shall be filled.

Matthew 5:6

A good appetite is usually a mark of good health. An individual who will not eat is generally thought to be ill. Even if a healthy person eats the wrong kinds of food, or develops irregular eating habits, he will become physically ill. These facts apply to spiritual hunger as well as to physical hunger. An individual who has no hunger for righteousness is spiritually ill. If the vision of what he might become does not stir him to desire earnestly these traits of the spirit, he is far from being happy.

It is obvious that before one can hunger and thirst after righteousness he must be poor in spirit. But not all those who are poor in spirit automatically hunger for righteousness. There are many individuals who are poor in spirit who have no yearning for spiritual food. Just as fasting dulls one's physical hunger, spiritual fasting dulls the appetite for spiritual things.

The righteousness of which Jesus spoke is a positive virtue. It is an attitude motivated by fatherly love. The eagerness of parents who are seeking ways to contribute to the happiness of their children is a good example of hungering and thirsting after righteousness. The only reward parents seek is that of being filled— that is, seeing their children healthy and happy. This beatitude does not urge men to desire spiritual things because it is their duty, but teaches them that happiness will come only when they have acquired a hunger and thirst for spirituality. Jesus here urges obedience to spiritual laws because they work to the advantage

19

of the one who masters them. The ways in which one's hunger for righteousness is expressed will be seen in the discussion of the other beatitudes.

Meekness

Happy are the meek: for they shall inherit the earth.

Matthew 5:5

The term "meekness" has acquired an unpleasant meaning, especially to the American mind. Some individuals have imagined that meekness is a spineless, groveling attitude, and that the meek person is the timid soul who is afraid to resist the wishes of others and therefore readily submits to them. This certainly was not the attitude that Jesus was teaching in the Sermon on the Mount. It was not Jesus who invented the phrase, "such a worm as I."

Since meekness is difficult to define, it would be well to give some examples of meekness. The prime example is the Master. When Jesus faced death on the cross he gave a magnificent example of meekness in his prayer in the Garden of Gethsemane: "If it be possible, let this cup pass from me; but, not my will but Thine be done." This willingness to subordinate his will to the will of God is meekness.

Moses presents another example of meekness. From the moment that he was called by God, he fought an almost impossible battle. But at all times he was bowing to the will of God. Moses refused to surrender his mission to the demands of expediency. At all times, with one exception, he subordinated his own wishes to the will of God. This is meekness.

Meekness is based on the unshakable faith that the universe is lawful. A scientist must come to nature with a meek attitude. He comes to nature to learn from it, and he quickly discovers that to learn from nature he must humble himself before the laws which govern the universe. Christian meekness is not only a faith that the universe is lawful; it is also a faith that Providence works for the good of God's children. Paul expressed a meek attitude when he wrote: "We know that in everything God works for good with those who love him, who are called according to his purpose" (Romans 8:28).

Meekness is not an easy attitude to learn. There are many temptations to rebel against God, and it is characteristic of human nature to want laws set aside. Many individuals have lost faith in God because he has not broken his laws for their sake. The meek individual trusts in the Providence of God even when he does

20

not understand it. He prays, "Thy will be done" even when this involves suffering. Job, who endured pain and agony without cursing God, is an example of the courage begotten by meekness.

Meekness, then, is a characteristic of a happy personality. The individual who has learned to subordinate his own will to that of God will find lasting happiness, and will truly inherit the earth. He is dedicated to a cause and devotes himself fully to it, even when it results in danger.

Purity of Heart

Happy are the pure in heart: for they shall see God.

Matthew 5:8

Purity of heart, like righteousness, has taken on a negative meaning. The pure in heart are thought to be those who do no wrong. As was true of righteousness, purity of heart is likewise more of a positive virtue than a negative one. Pure water is not only that without sediment and bacteria—it is good water which quenches thirst. Pure food is not simply that which lacks poison and contamination; it also nourishes and gives strength to the body. Purity of heart is not simply the lack of sin and evil. The pure in heart are those individuals who are dominated by a love of mankind.

Purity of heart enables one to see the best in people. Suspicion and distrust have no place in the pure heart. This was certainly the attitude of Jesus. When he looked at man he saw the best in them. It must have seemed foolish to those who knew the impulsiveness of Peter for Jesus to rename him the Rock. Yet, Jesus saw the potential and dynamic personality who would later become a pillar in the early church.

Purity of heart is certainly an attitude of fatherly love. A father always sees the best in his children. He does not close his eyes to their imperfections, but loves them for the good that is there. He knows them for what they can become. The opposite of purity of heart is the attitude of suspicion and distrust. An individual who cannot see the good in others is an unhappy person. He finds it easy to seek out the splinter in the personality of others although there is a timber in his own life. It is especially easy for an individual to discover flaws in the lives of those whom he dislikes, which illustrates that lack of purity of heart is due to a lack of love for others.

The pure in heart are always looking for the best in men, and they usually find it. When men love others as a father loves his children, they will discover that purity of heart naturally follows. The reward Jesus promised is a vision of God. To see God means to develop a strong bond of fellowship with him. The Greek word that is here translated "see" could equally well be translated "experience," as it is translated in Luke 2:26. The pure in heart experience God in a way that others do not. God, for them, is a living experience. He is someone with whom they are acquainted due to a life of service. This is the reward promised to the pure in heart.

Christian Education

The best kind of Christian education is that which seeks to instill these principles of happiness into the lives of children. The best education teaches children to be poor in spirit by urging them on to further development and growth. It urges a child never to be self-satisfied, but to press on to a vision of higher things. A wise parent instills within his child a hunger for righteousness by suggesting that learning is a privilege and is its own reward. Learning is not a drudgery to be endured, but a privilege to be sought. A wise parent teaches his child to be meek by instilling within him a firm faith in the Providence of God. He teaches him purity of heart by urging him to look for the best in others. A wise parent will set the proper example by refusing to talk about the unpleasant characteristics of others, and will urge his child not to talk about others behind their backs. He will teach his child that the men who have betrayed this trust are to be pitied rather than feared.

Faith is a tremendous force in the life of a Christian only if it is properly utilized. The principles of life called for in these four beatitudes demand more than a merely intellectual faith. They demand that one be wholly transformed by the renewal of his mind (Romans 12:2).

Questions

1. What are some of the ways men have sought happiness? From your own experience, give examples showing how unsuccessful some of these ways have been.
2. What was Jesus' method for finding happiness? Discuss the superiority of this method.
3. What are some of the ways that men today manifest poverty of spirit?

4. Give some examples of "wealth of spirit." Is the man who is always dogmatically confident he is right an example of wealth of spirit?

5. What essential human needs are thwarted by an attitude of "wealth of spirit"?

6. Why is it that some persons who are poor in spirit do not have a hungering for righteousness? What can be done to remedy this situation?

7. What are some of the popular definitions of meekness? What does the New Testament mean by meekness? How does this differ from the popular definitions?

8. Give some additional examples of meekness from the Bible. Give examples from the life of Paul illustrating his meekness. Would you classify Peter as a meek individual?

9. Did Christ look at purity of heart as a positive or negative virtue? How did Jesus manifest purity of heart? Give some examples.

10. What did Jesus mean when he said the pure in heart shall "see" God? What other meaning could the word "see" have in this context?

11. Since these attitudes are essential to a person's happiness, what are ways that parents can teach them to their children?

Chapter 3

The Power of Fatherly Love

"A NEW COMMANDMENT I give to you, that you love one another; even as I have loved you, that you also love one another" (John 13:34). With this commandment Jesus instituted a new ideal of conduct—that of fatherly love. The remaining four beatitudes accurately describe this fatherly love and show how a life of happiness results from the application of these principles.

Happiness in Mourning

Happy are they that mourn: for they shall be comforted.
Matthew 5:4

Common sense would never have suggested to men that happiness could come from mourning, yet Jesus stated this as an eternal truth. This at first sounds paradoxical, but the key to understanding what Jesus meant lies in the significance of the word "mourn." This particular word does not usually refer to the outward expressions of grief and sorrow; there was another Greek word for that. Instead, it expresses a sense of deep concern—often concern for the sins of others, as the word is used in 1 Corinthians 5:2.

In this context Jesus is not dealing with childish whining or the sorrow that results from personal loss. He is dealing with the same kind of loving concern that a parent has for his child: the anxiety that leads parents to rear a child to a happy and worthwhile manhood. He is talking about the kind of love which makes a man sensitive to the needs and failures of his children. This is the kind of love Jesus had for the rich young ruler (Matt. 19:16-22). Like a father, he saw the possibilities in the young man which he did not have the character to use. If one is to find true happiness, he must develop this kind of love for all mankind.

Juvenile authorities reveal that the reason for delinquency in young people is often a lack of sympathetic and understanding friendship from the child's elders. In almost every case there was no one who cared. Delinquents have no one to "mourn" for them, and the result is a twisted and unhappy life.

Man is by nature a social creature who is interested in those around him. Many students of the human mind insist that man is by nature sympathetic. If this is true, why is there so much callousness among individuals? Why cannot the hearts of men be quickened to the human need of others? The answer is that this noble concern for others has been repressed.

This is a tradition, especially among men, which has no official name but perhaps could best be called the "he-man" attitude. As soon as a boy can understand words, he is told "Boys don't cry!" During the years of his early learning, when he could be taught to strengthen and develop his natural concern for others, he is being taught to suppress his natural feelings. Instead of being taught the virtue of mourning for others, he is taught that to be a man he must suppress his emotions. He does this by first of all avoiding those situations which might arouse deep sympathy within him. He becomes afraid to see suffering. He also tries to harden his heart and suppress his sensitivity so that he will not cry when there is reason for it. The motivation behind this "boys don't cry" attitude is sincere, but it is the exact opposite of the teaching of Jesus.

Parents are naturally anxious for their sons to be courageous. But they have defeated their purpose by repressing one of the noblest traits of manhood. Look at the Bible for examples of men of great courage who mourned over the misfortune of others. If one were to make a list, it would include the names of Moses, Abraham, Samuel, David, Elijah, Jeremiah, Isaiah, Amos and Hosea. It can perhaps be seen best in Jesus, a perfect expression of courageous manhood. He was not afraid to have compassion on the multitudes, to express his deep concern over the fortune of Israel, or to cry at the death of a beloved friend. One of the most moving passages in the New Testament is "Jesus wept." On the other hand, examples of the real "he-man" would be Goliath, Joab and Samson.

Here again, Jesus is not stating an ethical command as much as he is stating an eternal principle. Concern for others bring lasting happiness. One characteristic of the sick personality is self-centeredness. The man who can lose himself in concern for others will not only be happier, he will be healthier as well. Parents should encourage their children to develop their natural sensitivity for others. They should teach children to show sympathy and should provide opportunities for them to express concern for the welfare of others.

Mercy

Happy are the merciful: for they shall obtain mercy.

Matthew 5:7

Many individuals have supposed that mercy is a passive and completely negative virtue by which one refrains from inflicting punishment on another person even though it is deserved. This is certainly not the kind of mercy urged by Jesus, for he taught that mercy is not a passive virtue but one that expresses itself in action. Mercy could be defined as the prevention of suffering in others, whether that suffering be mental or physical. Here again, fatherly love expresses itself in mercy. Parents try to foresee the hard knocks their children may meet. They try to save them from as many as possible, and give them strength to meet the others.

The best illustrations of Jesus' concept of mercy are found in his own life. He was merciful to the woman found in adultery when others would have stoned her to death. He not only told her "Neither do I condemn you," he also forgave her sins. To be merciful after the example of Jesus involves an attitude of forgiveness toward others.

Mercy makes it possible for one to love his enemies. Not only does the Christian refuse to strike back at those who have offended him, he forgives them as well. This is fatherly love at its best. When a child sins against a father, the father does not seek retribution. Instead, he forgives the child and longs to welcome him back into his embrace. The parable of the prodigal son supplies an excellent example of fatherly mercy.

It is not always easy to know how to be merciful. Parents agonize through sleepless nights searching for wisdom to keep their children from rushing into unhappiness and sorrow. Mercy does not always express itself by withholding punishment. Many times it is more merciful for a child to be spanked than to be spoiled. A teacher may discover that the most merciful action toward a student may be failing him, although the student is not likely to think so. Mercy is that attitude which has the welfare of the other person uppermost at all times. It is obvious that mercy can prevail only where fatherly love is the dominating motive of one's behavior.

The same methods used to teach a child concern for others can be used to teach him to be merciful. When one has learned to

26

mourn, that is, to be sympathetic to the needs of others, it will be natural for him to do something about it. Young children can be taught to be merciful toward younger children and toward animals. If a child is taught the attitude of mercy early in life, he will find that his adult years are happier and healthier. To teach a child by word or action to turn a deaf ear to the needs of others, or to teach him that the most important thing in life is his own welfare, is to condemn him to a life of frustration and unhappiness.

Peacemaking

Happy are the peacemakers: for they shall be called the sons of God.

Matthew 5:9

The Christian life brings the "peace that passes understanding" (Philippians 4:7). This is a peace, however, that must be pursued. One of the final statements Jesus made to his disciples was: "Peace I leave with you; my peace I give to you; not as the world gives do I give to you. Let not your hearts be troubled, neither let them be afraid" (John 14:27). This kind of peace involved not so much a change outside the man as a change within.

There are three basic attitudes which destroy peace. At the foundation of them is fear. Closely following are greed and anger. These three attitudes are responsible for conflict whether it be a struggle within an individual, a conflect between an individual and his society, or a conflict between nations. Sons of God must be peacemakers—not only because it is a duty, but also because it brings lasting happiness. If one will work to destroy fear, greed, and anger in his life, he will discover that peace is the inevitable result.

A young man in college felt he was being treated unfairly by his instructor. He was both afraid of failing the course and angry at the instructor because of the mistreatment. A friend pointed out that his quick resentment to injustice was a weakness in his character which could be overcome by the right attitudes. The young man determined in his heart to overcome his anger. This had a marked effect not only on the young man but upon the instructor as well. Curiously enough, the instructor not only ceased his unfair treatment of the boy, he also apologized for his former behavior. This young man discovered that when he resolved to overcome his fear and anger, his problem was soon solved so that dismay gave place to happiness. The way to conquer injustice is to overcome it with the fatherly love Jesus taught.

MOMENTS ON THE MOUNT

Happiness in Persecution

Happy are they which are persecuted for righteousness' sake: for theirs is the kingdom of heaven. Happy are ye, when men shall revile you, and persecute you, and shall say all manner of evil against you falsely, for my sake. Rejoice and be exceeding glad: for great is your reward in heaven: for so persecuted they the prophets which were before you.

Matthew 5:10-12

It is significant that Jesus followed his promise of peace with a statement regarding persecution. He knew that his disciples and countless thousands more would be persecuted because of their faith. Yet, he promised them an inner peace which would bring happiness. It is this peace that Paul, an old man lying in prison awaiting death, could write of to Timothy. The old soldier told the young evangelist: "For God did not give us a spirit of fear, but of power, and of love and self-control." Centuries later, when two Englishmen were about to be burned at the stake for righteousness' sake, one of them, Latimer, spoke to the other in these words: "Be of good cheer, Master Ridley, we shall this day light such a candle, by God's grace, in England, as I trust never shall be put out."

Jesus was not preaching asceticism. There is no indication in the New Testament that physical self-abasement produces godliness. In fact, Paul insisted that such things are of no value in checking the indulgence of the flesh (Col. 2:23). It was not that the disciples should seek injury for injury's sake, but that they were happy to serve Christ, even if suffering were necessary.

This is a characteristic of fatherly love. Jesus said, "Greater love hath no man than this, that a man lay down his life for his friends." A father would gladly lay down his life for his son and would be considered abnormal if he did not love his son enough to do it.

The joy of which Jesus spoke comes to the Christian even in the face of persecution. The Christian knows that his cause is worth suffering for—even dying for, and this brings him happiness in persecution. Children should be taught that the best motivation for courage is love. Christ courageously faced the cross because of his love for the world. His disciples courageously faced death because of their love for Christ and for his cause. It is this type of courage that brings happiness to the follower of Christ.

An important thing to notice in all eight of these beatitudes is the emphasis upon service to others. Jesus taught that if men will develop these attitudes toward others, they will achieve lasting happiness not only in this world but also in the world to come. One finds happiness for himself by seeking happiness for others. As Jesus stated this principle: "He who finds his life will lose it, and he who loses his life for my sake will find it" (Matt. 10:39).

Questions

1. What does the word "mourn" mean as used by Jesus in Matthew 5:4? Compare also James 4:8-9 and 2 Corinthians 12:21 where this same word is used.

2. Is fatherly love essential for the development of this kind of mourning? How do parents "mourn" for their children? What is their reward?

3. How is this concern for others repressed by the "boys don't cry" attitude? How is this attitude out of harmony with the teachings of Jesus?

4. What is the real source of courageous manhood? How does a suppression of one's concern for others produce a warped attitude? Give some examples from the Bible· of the real "he-man" attitude.

5. Did Jesus teach that mercy is a positive or negative virtue? How can mercy be expressed positively?

6. How does mercy reveal itself to be dependent upon the presence of fatherly love? In what ways do parents show mercy to their children?

7. How can parents teach their children to "mourn" for the welfare of others and to be merciful to others?

8. What kind of peace did Jesus promise to his disciples? Was this peace based on freedom from persecution? Compare especially John 14:27, 28.

9. What are the attitudes which destroy peace? How do the principles taught by Jesus help one overcome these attitudes?

10. Does the New Testament teach that severity to the body will produce godliness? See Colossians 2:23.

11. What attitude is necessary for faithfulness even in face of persecution. How does this attitude depend upon fatherly love? How does this bring joy?

Chapter 4

The Salt of the Earth

SOME CHRISTIANS think that the follower of Christ must seclude himself from the contamination of society and must not associate with unbelievers for fear of becoming corrupted. This idea is certainly not a Christian principle, as is shown by the following verses from the Sermon on the Mount:

> You are the salt of the earth; but if salt has lost its taste, how shall its saltiness be restored. It is no longer good for anything except to be thrown out and trodden under foot by men.
> You are the light of the world. A city set on a hill cannot be hid. Nor do men light a lamp and put it under a bushel, but on a stand, and it gives light to all in the house. Let your light so shine before men, that they may see your good works and give glory to your Father who is in heaven.
>
> Matthew 5:13-16

The story of salt in the history of mankind is an interesting one. In the Orient, during the time of Jesus, it was so valuable that soldiers often received part of their wages in salt. The word "salary" has its origin in this fact, as does the expression, "the man is worth his salt."

During the time of Jesus, salt was even more valuable than it is today, for it was about the only preservative available. It was also used as an antiseptic and was used then, as now, for flavoring purposes. Jesus was paying a high tribute to his disciples when he called them the "salt of the earth." They were expected to preserve the good qualities and high ideals of their society, and they were to add flavor to the lives of others by their influence.

Another characteristic of salt is that it never gains its ends by rejoicing in its own saltiness. It finds itself only by losing itself. Salt is valuable only when it is in the midst of things, making them taste better, preventing them from spoiling, or freeing them from corruption. Salt, by itself, unused, is worth very little.

The Salt of the Earth

When one speaks of well-flavored food he does not even mention the presence of salt. The meal is not well-flavored if one can taste the salt. Yet, how terrible food tastes without its flavoring power. As a preservative its value lies in the preservation of other things; never of itself. As an antiseptic its value lies in preventing the corruption of other things, for salt cannot of itself be destroyed.

It can, however, lose its saving, flavoring and preserving powers. When this happens it becomes worthless and is transformed from a boon to mankind to his curse. Instead of preserving, it destroys. One must even be careful when he discards it, for the ground upon which it falls will lose its fertility. This is the reason for casting it in the pathways where it can do no damage.

The second figure of speech Jesus used was that of light. Light, like salt, does not accomplish its purpose by calling attention to itself. Light is useless if its only function is to glare in the eyes of the one for whom it should serve as a light. It can serve as a guilding light only when it does not blind the eyes of the one for whom it shines.

The lesson that Jesus taught in these figures of speech is that the followers of Jesus should not live self-centered lives but should live in dedicated service to others. Yet, the temptation is always present for a Christian to shine so brilliantly in the eyes of those whom he leads that they are blinded to the Christ they claim to be following. This is as bad an error as the opposite extreme of hiding one's light under a bushel where it gives light to no one.

There is perhaps no better way in which Christians can apply these principles than in their daily work. The mistaken notion has arisen that the only individuals who really let their light shine before men are those persons who devote themselves to fulltime evangelistic and preaching work. This was not the teaching of Jesus here. He was not singling out the Christian minister for particular praise, but was showing how each Christian, regardless of his vocation in life, can be a living witness of Christ.

The Christian's Calling

Pride seems to be an occupational hazard of preachers. Like the light that blinds the eyes of a person who is trying to see the road, the preacher occasionally becomes so self-centered that it is difficult to see the light of Christ in his life. The Christian should never shine his own light, but only reflect the light of Christ.

In this context Jesus was talking about the businessman, the laborer, the housewife and the professional man. These individuals

31

can have as much good influence for Christ as any evangelist who ever lived—if they only apply in their lives the attitudes of heart that Jesus stressed in the beatitudes.

The key to one's life work is found in a passage which occurs later in the Sermon on the Mount. "Lay not up for yourselves treasures upon earth: but lay up for yourselves treasures in heaven." Paraphrased and applied to the choice of one's vocation it might read, "Do not pick out a life work in terms of individual profit, but in terms of righteous achievement." Parents could urge no higher goal upon their children than to become Christian businessmen. Christian lawyers, Christian doctors, Christian professors and Christian laborers. The individual driving a bulldozer will reach persons that the preacher in his pulpit will never contact. Men are needed in every phase of life who have not lost their own ideals, and who, through their influence and their moral integrity, are powerful in preserving high ideals in others. Like salt, they can preserve the good that is found in their associates. And like light, they can show the way to the Master.

Looked upon in this way, every Christian has a calling. He is called to be a living witness for Christ. Like the early disciples, Christians of today can be witnesses for Christ to the ends of the earth (Acts 1:8). When the gospel is taken to all the earth, it will largely be due to the efforts of Christian men and women who are scattered throughout the globe engaging in their various occupations.

Work need not be considered a drudgery and looked upon merely as a means of earning a living. It should rather be considered an opportunity to serve others and to bring the light of Christ into their lives. The dedicated Christian men and women who are laboring in the fields and factories of the nation are perhaps the most effective preachers. This attitude toward one's work makes even the monotonous tasks, which so often make life a drudgery into a chance for thrilling achievements. In any walk of life, one can find challenges to his best abilities if he has the vision of becoming the salt of the earth and the light of the world.

The Christian's Attitudes

The tragedy is that many Christians fail to be effective witnesses because they have never understood the key to abundant living. They have not developed in their own lives the attitudes which Jesus promised would bring happiness. Instead of spreading a radiant light, they project the image of an unhappy and dissatisfied personality. A long face, sour disposition and sharp tongue can never be effective means of winning others to Christ.

The contrast between the sour personality and the radiance of the abundant life is illustrated by Jesus who referred, in a humorous way, to the self-righteousness of the Pharisees. The Pharisees, as do many Christians today, tried to impress others with their piety by making a show of it. This generally took the form of long-faced attitudes and non-attractive appearances. Notice Jesus' denunciation of this type of piety.

> And when you fast, do not look dismal, like the hypocrites, for they disfigure their faces that their fasting may be seen by men. Truly, I say to you, they have their reward. But when you fast, annoint your head and wash your face, that your fasting may not be seen by men but by your Father who is in secret; and your Father who sees in secret will reward you."
>
> Matthew 6:16-18

The Christian personality should be attractive to others, not repulsive to them. Fortunately, the most important features of an attractive personality are those which are learned attitudes. Physical beauty and intelligence are assets, but they are by no means essential to an attractive personality. Everyone knows an individual who is physically attractive but spiritually unpleasant. The intellectual snob is as unpleasant to be around as is the man who berates education. The harmonious individual can use his physical beauty or intelligence in such a way to win others to Christ; but these are not the most essential elements in his personality.

By far the most important factor in an attractive personality is temperament. Temperament is the name given to the collection of attitudes which determine an individual's personality. A person's temperament is his attitude toward God. If most of a person's attitudes are fear attitudes, he will have a timid temperament. If he has a large number of anger habits, he is described as having a bad temper. If he has developed the attitudes which Jesus stressed in the beatitudes, he will have the Christian personality, the mark of a happy man.

A common misconception is that one's temperament is inherited. Students of the human mind have good reason to believe that this is not so. Much of a child's temperament is developed by the time he is three years of age and is patterned after the only teachers he has had—his parents. One can see the wisdom in Paul's admonition: "Fathers, do not provoke your children to anger, but bring them up in the discipline and instruction of the Lord" (Ephesians 6:4). A wise parent will seek to instill within his child the attitudes of heart that are taught in the beatitudes. He could give his child no greater gift than the key to a happy and abundant life.

"You are the salt of the earth and the light of the world." What powerful figures these are! Jesus used these figures to describe the power of the Christian personality. Regardless of one's vocation, he can make his life more useful by using his position to shed the light of Christ into the hearts of others. One who has developed the attitudes taught by Jesus can have a greater influence upon others because his personality is more attractive to them. Instead of being discontent and sour on the world, the Christian has every reason in the world to be happy. If he develops the attitudes of heart taught by Jesus, he will be able to truly let his light shine before men, that they may see his good works and give glory to God in heaven (Matthew 5:16).

Questions

1. Did Jesus teach that the Christian should completely separate himself from society? Was this Jesus' personal policy? See Matthew 9:10-13.
2. What central lesson did Jesus teach by the use of the figures of salt and light?
3. How is salt a good analogy for the duties of Christian influence? How can Christians act as salt to the world?
4. In what ways can Christians fail to shine the light of Christ? What are the attitudes that replace Christ's light with the light of one's own life?
5. How can Christians be lights to the world? Can those who are not evangelists be effective lights for their associates?
6. What is the result when one tries to shine his own light so brilliantly that he blinds one to the light of Christ? Why do preachers especially have to guard against this?
7. Does every Christian have a "calling"? What is the basis for deciding upon one's life's work?
8. What attitudes taught by Jesus transform work from a drudgery into an opportunity for service to others?
9. Why is it that many Christians fail to be effective witnesses? What attitudes make them unpleasant to others?
10. Are some church members guilty of the same false attitudes that Jesus condemned in the Pharisees? How do church members today seek to impress others with their piety?

11. What are the most important elements in an attractive personality? Can these attitudes be developed?
12. How can children be taught these necessary attitudes? Do they inherit them?

Chapter 5

The Development of Character

THE GREEK WORD "character" originally meant a tool for engraving, or the stamp or impress made upon something else, as the engraving on a coin. The word is used only once in the New Testament and then refers to Christ: "He reflects the glory of God and bears the very stamp (character) of his nature . . ." (Hebrews 1:3).

Character now popularly refers to a person's moral firmness or ethical vitality. A man's character determines the kind of person he is and the kind of attitudes he will have when faced with temptation. Since the development of strong character is essential to a happy life, each Christian should look to Christ for the key to character building attitudes.

Weakness or Character?

As soon as the problem of character development is considered, one is presented with the apparent paradox that the man who appears most attractive is not the one who is ethically flawless. The current attitude toward manhood is that if a person is to be a real "he-man" and not a "sissy," he must take a fling at sin. This attitude is reflected in advertisements and in the popular television hero who proves himself to be a man by his less than decent behavior. Because of this misconception, many young people in college feel that to be a part of the crowd and to show that they are really grown up they must engage in those activities they were taught to frown upon. Recently a young man made this comment: "I never drank before I came to college. I was quite a boy scout then." He made this comment in derision of his previous "innocence," and was quite proud that he had at last found freedom and maturity. What he failed to realize was that he was too weak to resist the temptations that confronted him, and instead of resisting them, as a man of strong character would, he gave in to them.

In spite of the popular attitude toward morality, society in general recognizes that its existence depends upon the moral integrity of its members. Society passes laws to discourage crime and criminals are punished. Here is the dilemma: parents want their children to be men and women of moral integrity; yet they do not want them to be prudish. How can they accomplish this end? One unfortunate solution some parents accept is to try to make their children just a little bit bad—just enough so they will be "human."

There are really two reasons for the notion that moral character and vitality are not compatible. The first of these is an identification of sensitivity with weakness. Many persons feel that a man who has a sensitive nature is not really masculine; this gives rise to the "boys don't cry" attitude that was discussed in chapter three. This attitude also insists that men should not really like poetry, art or religion, and those who do are really not "he-men." A man who possesses these basic sensitivities may try to downgrade them and may attempt to promote his "masculinity" by turning to profanity, drinking and other kinds of immorality. It is unfortunate that our culture has destroyed much potential for achievement by disgracing the man who has qualities of sensitivity. One should always carefully distinguish between the namby-pamby weakling and the sensitive man who in reality possesses some admirable characteristics.

The second reason for this attitude is the fact that people notice the exceptions to the rule rather than the majority behavior. To see the matter more clearly, one must admit that the vast majority of immoral persons are far from being admirable; they are weak individuals who are ruled by their own passions. They lie, cheat, steal and show no reverence for sacred things. Yet, there are some persons who imagine that immorality will make them manly because of the popular image suggested by television and the movies. They fail to realize that there are thousands of strong individuals who are strictly moral. The truth of the matter is that a majority of strong characters are moral and a majority of immoral characters are weak.

The motivation underlying this fear of being too good is a desire to be strong. It is here that the teachings of Jesus provide the key to strength which in turn produces manly character. Jesus taught that strong character is not produced by any kind of external behavior, but consists in the power which motivates one's actions.

It was this great truth that the Pharisees misunderstood. By focusing all their attention upon externalities, they missed the great power inherent in the law. Before chiding them for their hypocrisy, Jesus stated his attitude toward the law of Moses.

> Think not that I have come to abolish the law and the prophets;
> I have come not to abolish them but to fulfill them. For truly,
> I say to you, till heaven and earth pass away, not an iota, not a
> dot, will pass from the law until all is accomplished.
>
> Matthew 5:17-18

Jesus' criticisms were not of the law of Moses, but of the false interpretations given to it by the Pharisees. The law itself had many spiritual qualities that were totally overlooked by the legalistically minded Pharisees (Romans 7:14). Jesus provided the perfect fulfillment of the law by urging men on to a higher morality: that of fatherly love.

Emphasis Upon Little Things

The attitude of Jesus toward the development of character is seen best in his attitude toward little things. He looked upon the law of Moses as a sacred covenant not to be treated lightly in any of its aspects.

> Whoever then relaxes one of the least of these commandments
> and teaches men so, shall be called least in the kingdom of heaven;
> but he who does them and teaches them shall be called great in
> the kingdom of heaven."
>
> Matthew 5:19

The next verse adds a further condemnation of the perverse religion of the Jewish legalists.

> For I tell you, unless your righteousness exceeds that of the
> scribes and Pharisees, you will never enter the kingdom of heaven."
>
> Matthew 5:20

These verses, at first reading, seem to indicate that the Pharisees were condemned because they left undone the little details of the law, and that Jesus was urging his disciples to be more scrupulous in keeping the details of the law than the scribes and Pharisees had been. An analysis of the other teachings of Jesus reveals this to be the exact opposite of what Jesus was saying. The religion of the Pharisees was so characterized by observance of the minute details of the law that they had completely overlooked the more important matters.

> Woe to you, scribes and Pharisees, hypocrites! for you tithe mint and dill and cummin, and have neglected the weightier matters of the law, justice and mercy and faith; these you ought to have done, without neglecting the others. You blind guides, straining out a gnat and swallowing a camel!
>
> Matthew 23:23-24

The point that Jesus was making is that when the proper spiritual attitudes are present, outward behavior will come as a matter of course. The Pharisees proceeded on the opposite assumption. They insisted that if one kept all the outward details of the law, goodness would follow.

The remarkable characteristic of the teachings of Jesus is that he never offered outward rules of behavior. His moral teaching was always in terms of inner attitudes. Yet, how often has the church's educational program been built around the same attitudes the Pharisees possessed. Many Bible classes focus attention on nothing but outward rules of behavior—a series of "do's" and "don't's." The result of this kind of education is that too often young people fail to develop the strong inner character that will give them the strength to wisely regulate their behavior.

Jesus recognized that the only way to change a person is to change his attitudes. Many young people in college "lose their faith" because they have never been taught the strong inner attitudes that will guide them in a situation which calls for strong character. Being away from the restraints to behavior provided by parents and by the church, the soon reveal that they do not have the inner character to properly use their newly gained freedom.

The principle taught by Jesus is that if one develops strong character, his behavior will be moral. If he neglects the development of his character, he will be a failure in his attempt to live the Christian life. Far too many Christians are good, not because they are thoroughly inspired by justice and mercy and faith, but because they are afraid to be bad. These characters do not have the strength to weather the storm of temptation that will eventually come.

Little Attitudes

Most Christians today have no trouble with what are commonly termed "major sins," murder, adultery, theft, and such things. Most Christians find the greatest challenge to morality in their little attitudes. Jesus recognized that the development of strong moral character depends upon one's attitude toward these "little" things. He insisted that anger sows the seeds of murder and that lust gives rise to adultery. His emphasis was upon attitudes of heart which can reap tragic results.

A particular example of this is his teaching in reference to truthfulness.

> Again you have heard that it was said to the men of old, 'You shall not swear, falsely, but shall perform to the Lord what you have sworn.' But I say unto you, Do not swear at all, either by heaven, for it is the throne of God, or by the earth, for it is his footstool, or by Jerusalem, for it is the city of the great King. And do not swear by your head, for you cannot make one hair white or black. Let what you say be simply 'Yes' or 'no'; anything more than this comes from evil.
>
> Matthew 5:33-37

Some Christians have understood Jesus to be saying here that oaths, as such, are sinful; some individuals still refuse to take an oath in court because they believe this teaching forbids it. A careful study of the attitude of heart here being condemned will reveal that Jesus was really warning against falsehoods in any form.

The Jews were accustomed to a gradation of oaths. Jesus sternly rebuked them for this in Matthew 23:16-22. The Pharisees said, "If any one swears by the temple, it is nothing; but if any one swears by the gold of the temple, he is bound by his oath." Another ploy was to say, "If anyone swears by the altar, it is nothing; but if anyone swears by the gift that is on the alter, he is bound by his oath." This is like the childish game of saying that something did not count "because I had my fingers crossed."

It was this attitude toward the truth that Jesus sternly condemned. A man's word should be the truth even when it is not backed up by an oath. How perverse it is for a man's word to be worth so little that he has to affirm the truthfulness of his statement by an oath. It was the evil attitude that made oaths necessary that Jesus condemned.

Although men rarely use oaths today, there is a similar malady that betrays a sinful attitude. This attitude is that of having different standards of truth for different occasions. The "white lie" is an illusion of the same thing Jesus condemned in the Pharisees. Another example is the attitude on the part of some church members that certain things are right in politics or in business that are wrong in other contexts. The man who tries to justify his shady dealing by saying that "business is business" is guilty of the same wicked attitude displayed by the Pharisees. The man in public office who tries to justify his actions by asserting that it is just "part of the game" is as severely condemned as is the man who tells a blatant falsehood.

How can parents teach their children truthfulness? By presenting them with proper examples. Children do not have to be taught to tell the truth. Many children have embarrassed their parents by telling the truth, when the parents might have wished that less than the truth had been revealed. A child may need to learn that in society there are occasions when the bald truth would be brutal and therefore fundamentally dishonest, but he cannot be taught truth on a sliding scale. He can be taught the attitude of truthfulness best by seeing reverence for the truth in the actions of his father and mother. For a mother to instruct a child to tell a caller that she "is not in" will do more to destroy reverence for truth in a child than can be corrected by all the mouth washing and physical punishments ever inflicted.

To develop strong character in a child parents must recognize the principles Jesus taught in the passages just studied.

1) True strength depends not upon outward actions but upon inner dispositions. The person who thinks that to be strong he must be immoral has a warped and distorted sense of strength.

2) Proper education does not concentrate on the external modes of behavior but upon the development of inner attitudes. The wise parent sees to it that his child develops the strength of character that will enable him to deal with problems even when he is separated from the restraints of his home and family life.

3) Finally, parents should recognize that the best way to teach proper attitudes is by presenting strong examples of these attitudes in their own lives. The parent who thinks that he can teach his child one thing and practice another will wonder 15 years later why his child went wrong, and will probably blame it on the schools or the church instead of himself.

Questions

1. What was the original meaning of the word "character"? To what specifically does the word now refer? How is this similar to its original meaning?
2. Why do many persons feel that the individual who is most attractive is not the one who is ethically flawless? What attitudes constitute a "he-man" personality as far as many individuals are concerned?

3. Discuss the idea that sensitivity is the same as weakness.
4. What motivates people to fear being "too good"?
5. What are two approaches to character building? Which one did Jesus teach?
6. What was Jesus' attitude toward the law of Moses? Did he treat it with disrespect? What is implied in his willingness to fulfill it? How did he fulfill it?
7. What did Jesus mean when he urged his disciples to exceed the righteousness of the scribes and Pharisees? Was he urging them to be more scrupulous in observance of the ceremonial demands of the law?
8. What principles did Jesus teach were the basis for moral behavior? Did he offer outward rules of behavior as a basis for moral action?
9. What effect might a "do" and "don't" type of teaching program have on young people? Why is such a program not the best kind of teaching program? Is this type of program in line with the principles Jesus taught?
10. Did Jesus forbid oaths as such? What about when a person swears in court to "tell the whole truth and nothing but the truth so help me God"? Does this violate Jesus' command?
11. What are some modern attitudes toward the truth that are similar to the attitudes the Pharisees had toward truthfulness?
12. What is the best way for parents to teach their children reverence for the truth?

Chapter 6

Natural Appetites

ONE OF THE indications of a lack of moral strength in modern society is its lax attitude toward divorce. Statistics reveal that in the United States, an average of one out of every three marriages ends in the divorce court. This fact certainly indicates that something is tragically wrong with modern society's attitude toward marriage in general and with sex in particular. It is not surprising that Jesus devoted a considerable part of the Sermon on the Mount to this subject.

Physical Desires

One cannot talk about marriage without talking about love. But in modern society, the terms "lust" and "love" are often confused. In the New Testament, the Greek word which is usually translated "lust" is used in many places to refer to any kind of unbridled and selfish desire—as is the case in Romans 6:12. Whenever any urge becomes strong enough to dominate one's entire personality, it can be described as lust. This is true whether one's lust is for fame, fortune or physical pleasure. In condemning the attitude of heart which promotes overt acts of sin, Jesus was striking at the very heart of the problem which is that of unbridled desires.

Whether parents admit it or not, sex is one of the most difficult problems a young person must face. Biologically, sex is the second strongest appetite. It is exceeded only by hunger as the most powerful motivating force in human behavior. Recognizing this fact, advertising men use the appeal of this appetite to persuade young people to purchase everything from hats to automobiles. The motion picture industry in turn has glorified the physical aspects of marriage to such an extent that many young people see only this side of marriage. It should not come as a surprise to modern parents when their children, who are exposed to these influences, are confused and concerned.

Jesus, who knew the needs and hearts of men better than anyone who ever lived, attacked the problem of physical desires in the following way:

> You have heard that it was said, "You shall not commit adultery. But I say to you that everyone who looks at a woman lustfully has already committed adultery with her in his heart."
>
> Matthew 5:27, 28

In his characteristic manner, Jesus emphasized the development of a strong inner character which will result in the avoidance of the outward sin. A man who refrains from adultery but lusts in his heart has not even begun to overcome his basic problem.

One significant thing to note is that Jesus is not condemning man's physical appetites. Any religion that ignores man's basic needs is perverse. The Bible has much to say about sex, but one thing that it never says is that this appetite is wrong or sinful. Jesus describes as "lust" this particular appetite when it is uncontrolled; any appetite can become sinful when it dominates one's personality. Parents make a tragic mistake when they rear children to believe that sex is the very essence of evil, or that there is something dirty and unclean about this natural human appetite.

There are four ways that an individual may go about satisfying his natural desires. This is true of all human desires, not just the sexual appetite. The first way is for an individual to ignore the edicts of society and give uncontrolled expression to his desires. This results, in the long run, in unhappiness, and maladjustments. The person who lets his desires control him is the worst kind of a slave, for he is controlled by forces that should be his servants, not his master.

A second way of dealing with natural desires is to repress them. The person who represses his appetites not only refuses to express them, he does not even admit that he has them. This is basically a form of dishonesty for the person who represses his desires is trying to deceive himself. The worst tragedy is that he cannot control them for he refuses to be truthful to himself. But in addition, students of the human mind insist that one cannot really put desires out of his mind—he only pushes them deeper into his mind and out of consciousness. Whenever one represses a desire, this desire becomes a part of his unconscious behavior and it does not express itself in the normal way. Physicians recognize the fact the repressed feelings or memories can cause physical maladies such as nervous disorders and various mental problems.

A third way of meeting one's desires is to suppress them. The person who accepts this solution experiences a desire, recognizes that he cannot fulfill it, and inhibits it. He neither expresses it nor represses it. This is a much healthier attitude than that of repression because it is an honest attitude.

A fourth way in which desires may be dealt with is to take the power of the drives which lead into unacceptable channels and throw them into acceptable ones. This is an honest attitude. It admits that the desire is present, but seeks to redirect it. For example, two elderly ladies, who never married, work in the same institution. One of them says she never wanted to marry and never saw the man she would have. But her actions betray her inner feelings. She behaves in a silly manner and is especially attentive to any man who comes near her. She becomes an object of amusement to her friends for they know that she has deceived herself. This is an example of repression. She will not face the facts.

The other woman feels that marriage is the natural state for a woman and frankly states that she is sorry she has never married. But since she has not, she throws her whole energy into her work. The results are that she is healthy in mind and is an influence for good wherever she is. This is an example of a person suppressing an appetite in such a way that will produce positive action.

Which of these solutions did Jesus teach? Certainly Jesus did not urge that one give vent to his desire, nor did he teach that one should refuse to admit that he has natural desires and appetites. The very fact that Jesus did such strong teaching on these subjects is an admission that the problems exist. Jesus' attitude toward natural desires is summed up in the following quotation:

> If your right eye causes you to sin, pluck it out and throw it away; it is better that you lose one of your members than that your whole-body be thrown into hell. And if your right hand causes you to sin, cut it off and throw it away; it is better that you lose one of your members than that your whole body be thrown into hell.

Matthew 5:29, 30

In this verse Jesus admits the power of man's natural urges and the difficulty of completely overcoming them. It should be noted that this verse follows immediately upon the passages that refer to lustful desire and is in direct reference to one's sexual appetite. If one cannot lawfully fulfill his desires, as in marriage, then the teachings of Jesus are that he must avoid those things which arouse within him those desires he is not prepared to fulfill.

If a person's recreation or the literature that he reads arouse within him the desires that he cannot fulfill, he had better cut these things off and cast them from him. This does not mean that a person should remove himself from society, but that it is better "that one member should perish, than that the whole body should be cast into hell." If his associates are causing him to be tempted to do things that are wrong, Jesus urges the man to "cast them from him."

This principle is true not only in reference to one's sexual desires but to any desire. A man who is trying to stop drinking must stay away from persons and places that tempt him to drink; and he must also form other acquaintances and develop other activities that make this easier. If a man finds that his job places him in the wrong company, he had better "cast" his job from him rather than lose his soul.

For the person who is unmarried, this is by far the most practical teaching possible. Instead of being torn by guilt and tormented by unfulfilled desires, it is far better to avoid those acquaintances and those situations which will make it harder to resist the forces of those drives. The teachings of Jesus are always practical and will lead to happiness for the one who follows them. It may not be easy to carry out this formula for dealing with one's physical desires, but the result will be worth the effort, for modern psychology has shown that a person who follows this teaching will be happier and will have a better outlook on life.

Divorce

The problem of divorce is closely related to the problem of adultery, which is why Jesus considered them in logical succession.

> It was also said, "Whoever divorces his wife, let him give her a certificate of divorce." But I say to you that everyone who divorces his wife, except on the ground of unchastity, makes her an adulteress; and whoever marries a divorced woman commits adultery."
> Matthew 5:31, 32

The divorce problem was as bad, if not worse, in Jesus' day as it is now. One group of Jews insisted that adultery was the only proper cause of divorce. Another group of Jews, who followed the teaching of Rabbi Hillel, allowed divorce for almost any reason at all including what might be called "incompatibility" in modern terminology, for they permitted divorce even if a wife should burn her husband's dinner. Divorce with them was as easy as it is in some localities today. In Rome, divorce was so common that it is said that women reckoned time by the number of husbands they had.

A more detailed statement of Jesus' teaching on divorce is found in Mark 10:3-9. Here he revealed that the law of Moses allowed divorce because of the hardness of their hearts but that from the beginning God decreed that what he had joined together man should not put asunder. In this passage Jesus stated that it was natural for man to seek marriage, for "from the beginning of creation, 'God made them male and female,' For this reason a man shall leave his father and mother and be joined to his wife, and the two shall become one" (Mark 10:6, 7). Therefore, there ought not to be any divorce.

It should be remembered, however, that Jesus strongly emphasized that lust is the basic problem; adultery is but its expression and divorce the result. Jesus here revealed a truth that modern psychology discovered in its own way: divorce is due to the predominance of a dominating urge. A girl may lust for money. If she does, marriage to a man without it is almost certain to fail. She may lust for social position or beauty. If she does, a marriage which does not produce them cannot succeed for her. A man may lust for social position and success in his business. If his wife does not contribute to this, he may soon want to divorce her.

Jesus taught that the basic reason for divorce is simply a lack of love. One does not hear of a good mother resigning her motherhood because of incompatibility with her children. In the Old Testament, Hosea illustrated how this type of love can be applied to marriage. Even though his wife was unfaithful to him, he took her back into his home and tried to reform her and promised forgiveness. If men and women will develop fatherly love, as taught by Jesus in the Sermon on the Mount, the problem of divorce will be solved.

Questions

1. How is the word "lust" used in the New Testament? Can a person lust for things which are good in themselves?
2. What are the strongest human appetites? Does the New Testament teach that these desires are wrong in themselves?
3. What are the four ways of dealing with natural desires? Which of these ways are unhealthy?
4. How did Jesus indicate a person is to control his physical appetites? Did he only condemn the outward manifestation of sin?

5. What does it mean to suppress a physical appetite? Why is this an honest attitude? Give some examples of this attitude?
6. Reread Matthew 5:29, 30. What are some ways that a person can "cast from him" those things that cause temptation? How is this to be understood in relation to one's natural appetites?
7. Why did the law of Moses allow divorce (Mark 10:3-9)? Was the divorce situation as bad in Jesus' day as it is today?
8. What is the basic cause for divorce?
9. What is the solution to the problem of divorce?

Chapter 7

Sources of Power

WORSHIP IS A vital part of the Christian faith, and the Christian is deprived of great sources of spiritual strength without proper worship. The Christian who absents himself from worship services will be the weaker for it because he is being deprived of spiritual power. In a similar way, the person who worships improperly will fail to gain the strength that can come from correctly motivated worship.

In the next section of the Sermon on the Mount, Jesus deals with the false and hypocritical forms of worship that were practiced by certain of the Pharisees. He often chided them for their hypocrisy and false attitudes, imploring their double standards and legalstic traditions. Concerning those who worshiped falsely he said, "You hypocrites! Well did Isaiah prophesy of you when he said: 'This people honors me with their lips, but their heart is far from me; in vain do they worship me, teaching as doctrines the precepts of men'" (Matthew 15:7-9).

Theatrical Worship

The first verse of the sixth chapter of Matthew declares the basic criticism Jesus waged against the hypocritical forms of worship that he saw all around.

> Beware of practicing your piety before men in order to be seen by them; for then you will have no reward from your Father who is in heaven."
>
> Matthew 6:1

The criticism Jesus made was of the Pharisees' motives for worship.

There are many motives which cause people to worship and Jesus indicated that some of them are wrong. Many individuals view worship as a kind of superstitious rite. They drone through the songs and prayers with never a thought as to the meaning of what they are saying. Their worship has about as much spiritual value as does the Hindu's prayer wheel, which he mechanically turns thinking it will impart to him some kind of mystical value. Worship for these persons is approached with much the same attitude used in nailing a horseshoe over a door to bring luck.

Another group of individuals worship for the same reason the Pharisees worshiped—"to be seen of men." The phrase "to be seen" comes from the Greek word *theathanai* from which the English word *theatrical* is derived. There is much worship that is merely theatrical, and some individuals go to church, buy a house or choose a car merely "to be seen of men." They would be horrified to be seen in worship services in anything but the most stylish clothes, and they insist that the church building be large and extravagant so it will make a good impression upon the neighborhood.

Jesus made it plain that worship "to be seen of men" does not bring a spiritual reward, although he was aware that it did bring a reward of sorts. The person who seeks social approval for his actions will be motivated to avoid certain temptations, but his main reward will be social approval, which is far from being the source of spiritual power that true worship provides.

On the other extreme are those individuals who pretend to scorn social approval and are negativistic in their behavior. These individuals are worshiping "to be seen of men" just as are those who seek social approval. When a person seeks social disapproval, he usually is compensating for an unconscious fear that he cannot get social approval. His reward, then, is in saving his pride from being wounded by failure.

The tragedy is that many individuals who are worshiping "to be seen of men" are unaware of it. Due to the human capacity for rationalization, they have convinced themselves that they are worshiping for motives that are other than the real ones. Rationalization might be defined as doing what one wants to do and then finding a good excuse for having done it. All individuals are guilty of rationalization to some degree, and some excuses are a form of it. The student who watches television all evening instead of studying offers as his excuse, "all work and no play makes Jack a dull boy." The person who misses worship services and then blames it on the fact that he "didn't feel well" is just covering up the real reason.

The best way to avoid rationalizations is to be as honest with oneself as possible. Perhaps the main reason the publican went home justified rather than the Pharisee was because he was aware of his true motives and the Pharisee was not. The publican was aware that he was a sinner; his worship was the outpouring of a heart burdened with sin. The Pharisee was anxious to let other men know how good he was and he used prayer as a rationalization for doing this. Notice that Jesus does not question the sincerity of the Pharisee. He may have been perfectly sincere. Yet, because his motives were wrong, his worship was hypocritical.

All church members are guilty of wrong motives which have been disguised by rationalizations. A minister who attends corrupt movies because he insists he must know what to preach against is rationalizing for his behavior. A mother who insists upon working and leaving her children with someone else may insist that she is doing it for financial reasons, when the real reason may be that she does not want to face up to the responsibilities of motherhood. The man who refuses to take a firm stand on moral issues because he says that one should not parade his righteousness is probably rationalizing for his behavior. The man who refuses to attend services because he does not like the sermons has simply provided an excuse for his behavior when the real reason is something else.

Jesus indicated that spiritual power could come through proper worship. The "reward from your Father who is in heaven" is the strength that only the true worshiper knows. The person who feels that merely going through the form of worship is enough has failed to grasp the meaning of these teachings of Jesus. In the succeeding verses of the sermon, Jesus considered three types of worship: almsgiving, fasting and prayer. A study of these will reveal the rewards that come to the true worshiper.

Almsgiving

Some individuals feel that giving is not really worship but is only a religious duty. Jesus indicated that spiritual rewards could come from the proper attitude in almsgiving. He also stressed that hypocritical attitudes in this act of worship produce no spiritual power.

Thus, when you give alms, sound no trumpet before you, as the hypocrites do in the synagogues and in the streets, that they may be praised by men. Truly I say to you, they have their reward. But when you give alms, do not let your left hand know what

your right hand is doing, so that your alms may be in secret; and
your Father who sees in secret will reward you.

Matthew 6:2-4

Almsgiving was an important part of the Jewish religion. To
the legalistic Pharisee, tithing was a religious exercise that served
as a form of protection, a sort of good luck token. It was customary for a Jew who wanted forgiveness for some sin to do pen-
ance in the form of almsgiving. One of the common ways was to
buy a skin of water and give it to the poor. Water was scarce in
Palestine and was usually obtainable only at great effort. It was
so precious that it was sold by water carriers on the street. Whenever a rich person purchased a skin of water for the poor, the
water carrier would stand in the street shouting and sounding a
trumpet, "O thirsty, come for a drink offering." The poor who
accepted this charity paid for it by heaping good wishes upon
the giver, such as "God, forgive thy sins, O giver of drink."
From this type of almsgiving the giver received quite a bit of
free advertising, and supposedly some forgiveness.

Jesus stated that these individuals had their reward. This reward was the pleasure obtained from thanks and flattery. Their
reward was from men, not the spiritual power that comes from
the Father.

This type of almsgiving is still quite fashionable. Many individuals would never have contributed to worthwhile benevolent
causes had they not been able to receive some kind of public
recognition. To have their names mentioned publicly, or to have
buildings named for them, or to receive plaudits from others is
their reward.

It should be noted that Jesus is not decrying fame and glory,
but he is objecting to these as motives for worship. When Jesus
said, "do not let your left hand know what your right hand is
doing," he was insisting that the fact of almsgiving should not
only be in secret from other men but even from the giver himself.
Many Christians have understood this verse to forbid making a
public show of benevolence, but they make a private show instead.
These individuals feel that there is more reward in giving privately
and are proud of their superior righteousness. To Jesus, this is
just as far from the spirit of true worship as is the ostentatious
show of the Pharisees.

"Do not let your left hand know what your right hand is doing."
One can suspect that Jesus was engaging in some of his characteristic humor. What did Jesus mean? Perhaps these two illustra-

tions will help. Here is a man who is asked to give to a benevolent cause. He believes that he must give according to his abundance, but not more, so he gives only what he can "afford." He pulls his money from his purse with his right hand and counts it carefully; this requires the cooperation of his left hand. In this case, his left hand knows what his right hand is doing.

As a second illustration consider a man whose child needs medical attention. What is his motivation for giving? Obviously it is his love for his child. When providing for his child, the father simply reaches in his pocket for all that is there. His difficulty is not to divide it according to his ability to give. If he used his left hand at all it was to reach into his other pocket to see if there were any more money there. This is fatherly love. This is the motivation for true worship in almsgiving. Paul said: "If I give away all that I have, and if I deliver my body to be burned, but have not love, I gain nothing" (1 Corinthians 13:2).

One occasionally hears the plea, "give until it hurts." This plea is based upon the assumption that one must give more than he really thinks he can "afford" before he receives spiritual value from it. The result is probably that the person basks in his own self-righteousness for making such a sacrifice that he is in reality giving "to be seen of men." Notice that Jesus never made such a demand upon his followers. The Christian point of view is not "give until it hurts," but rather, "give until the need is met."

Parents make a tragic mistake when they force their children to give to others when the spirit is lacking. Although their motivation is sincere, these parents feel that the outward action of giving will promote the inner spirit of love for the needs of others. Jesus showed that this is not true. A child should be motivated to love others enough to want to share whatever he has with them. To teach a child to love children of other lands enough to give to foreign missions is far better than insisting that he contribute because it is his duty.

Fasting

Whenever a list of acts of worship is made, fasting is notably absent. Yet, there can be no denying that Jesus recognized the power of fasting as worship. He not only commanded proper attitudes in fasting, he also practiced it in his personal life.

And when you fast, do not look dismal, like the hypocrites, for they disfigure their faces that their fasting may be seen by men. Truly, I say to you, they have their reward. But when you fast, anoint your head and wash your face, that your fasting may not be seen by men but by your Father who is in secret; and your Father who sees in secret will reward you.

Matthew 6:10-18

Fasting as practiced by the Jews, involved a voluntary deprivation from food for a period of time. Fasting was practiced for two reasons. Some individuals fasted as a rite and as a demonstration of his faithfulness. As Jesus indicated, it was more often than not practiced "to be seen of men." There was nothing secret about it, for the Pharisees made sure that others could recognize their fasting by the pained expressions and unwashed faces.

Although Christians today do not deprive themselves of food, they do "fast" in ways similar to the ostentatious displays of the Pharisees. The over-worked minister who constantly impresses upon his congregation that he is worked to death is an example of a modern form of "fasting." The housewife who assumes a harassed look and spends much of her time impressing upon the rest of the household how oppressive her duties are and how much she needs rest and sympathy is another example of modern "fasting." Both individuals have their reward.

The second motivation for fasting was that it permitted a long period of deep meditation. This was the kind of fasting Jesus did. At the beginning of his ministry he fasted forty days. Before a time of great spiritual effort, he received renewed strength through fasting. It was not for him an outward ceremonial but an expression of his concern for higher values. Jesus objected to making fasting a ritual. Indeed, he and his disciples often ignored Jewish ceremonial, and were criticized for it.

When Jesus went into the wilderness for forty days in preparation for his temptation, he was pondering the nature of his mission and the challenges it would offer. Therefore, when he was tempted to eat, bread seemed pitifully unimportant. It is this dedication to spiritual values that makes the mundane demands of life seem so trivial. Only when a person becomes so caught up in serving the needs of others that he takes no time for such insignificant things as food can one say he has received spiritual benefit from fasting.

A father ministering to the needs of his sick daughter will be totally unconcerned about his personal needs. Many a father has spent sleepless nights and days without food because his concern for the welfare of his children pushed all other concerns from his mind. A father who sits beside the bed of his sick child is totally unconcerned about anything as unimportant as food. Again it can be seen that fasting is characteristic of fatherly love.

The preacher who spends a sleepless night before delivering a message that weighs heavily on his heart has captured the true power that comes from fasting. The man whose dedication to a cause makes his own welfare seem trivial, who gains strength from dedication to his work, has discovered the power that comes through fasting.

True worship, as taught by Jesus, emphasizes inner attitudes, not outward forms. Through a cultivation of the proper motives for worship, one can receive spiritual strength to meet the trials that will inevitably come. A person who learns the true spirit of worship will discover that he has tapped a vast reservoir of spiritual power.

Questions

1. Why was the worship of the Pharisees unacceptable? What was the major motive for their worship? What kind of a reward did this produce?
2. What is meant by "theatrical worship"? What modern attitudes make worship theatrical? Does this kind of worship bring a reward? What kind of a reward?
3. What is meant by rationalization? Give some examples of rationalization? Are most excuses forms of rationalizations?
4. How can one avoid being dishonest with himself? Compare here the respective attitudes of the Pharisee and the publican.
5. Give some additional examples of ways in which church members rationalize their behavior.
6. Why should almsgiving be considered as worship?
7. What are the proper motives for almsgiving? What are some improper motives for almsgiving? Give some examples.
8. Did Jesus condemn a public show of giving while approving a private show in benevolent activity?
9. What did Jesus mean by his command not to let the left hand know what the right hand is doing? Give some additional illustrations of this.
10. Is the principle "give until it hurts" a Christian point of view? What is the Christian demand for giving?
11. How do modern individuals "fast"?
12. How is fasting dependent upon fatherly love?

Chapter 8

Power Through Prayer

THE REASON many Christians do not have the strength to meet the trials they experience is that they have never tapped one of the greatest sources of spiritual strength—prayer. Prayer, like the forms of worship discussed in the last chapter, can be drained of its spiritual power by a misunderstanding of the proper motivation for prayer. It was because of their improper motives that Jesus condemned the prayers of the Pharisees.

> And when you pray you must not be like the hypocrites; for they love to stand and pray at the synagogues and at the street corners, that they may be seen by men. Truly I say to you, they have their reward. But when you pray, go into your room and shut the door and pray to your Father who is in secret; and your Father who sees in secret will reward you.
>
> And in praying do not heap up empty phrases as the Gentiles do; for they think that they will be heard for their many words. Do not be like them, for your Father knows what you need before you ask him.
>
> Matthew 6:5-8

How to pray is a problem that is as old as humanity. The disciples keenly felt their inability to pray, and asked their Lord to instruct them. The modern individual, suddenly faced with a critical need and painfully aware of his lack of resources to meet that need, may become conscious of his inability to pray. Then he too will stand with the disciples and say, "Lord, teach us to pray."

Why Should One Pray?

There are as many motivations for prayer as there are types of prayer. There is the childish notion of God as a super-Santa Claus who will give whatever he is asked for. Some individuals never outgrow this childish attitude. The only prayer they can pray is: "Lord, thank you for your blessings; please bless me some more." To compare this with the profound utterances of the prayers of Jesus should make them aware of their need for instruction in how to pray.

There are other individuals who pray only when they are in trouble. They feel no need for God's helping hand until they are faced with sudden danger. Then terror strikes at their hearts and they pray more out of desperation than for any other reason. Prayers like this rarely increase the spiritual strength of the individual, for when the danger passes, he forgets to pray until he is again faced with a situation which he cannot handle by his own resources.

Then there are those who pray "to be seen of men." Their reward is just as superficial as is the reward of those who give alms or fast in order to parade their piety. In contrast to this, Jesus urged his disciples to pray in their inner chamber. Public prayer may sometimes be as much in the inner chamber of the heart of the one who is praying as though he were in the darkest cellar. Prayer should express the heartfelt needs of the individual who is pouring out his petitions to his Father in heaven. This is a prayer that is prayed "in secret."

The Gentiles thought that their prayers would be heard if they were long and pompous. Jesus insisted that trying to gain an audience with God by shouting "Lord, Lord" will not insure success. Jesus practiced this ideal in his own life, for whenever he prayed in public, his prayers were short and meaningful. When he prayed in private, however, he prayed all night.

If a person will contrast his prayers with the prayers of Jesus, he will discover that many of his prayers are selfish, pompous, thoughtless or platitudinal. Many Christians have not progressed beyond the childish stage of thanking God for his blessings and asking for more. How many Christians ask for the secrets of transforming personality, for insights into the demands of the kingdom of heaven, or for strength to meet spiritual crises? One who realizes his need for the power that comes through prayer can well ask with the disciples, "Lord, teach us to pray."

When he gave a model prayer, Jesus did not intend for his disciples to use it as a liturgical formula. To pray the Lord's prayer does not mean that one should merely repeat it as if there were some magical value obtained from merely repeating the words. If one is to truly profit from this model prayer, he must understand the attitudes of heart that are necessary for the one who prays an acceptable prayer. The Lord's model prayer requires depth of character and sincerity of heart on the part of the one who prays acceptably. Almost any flaw in one's character makes some part of it impossible to pray. If a person is angry with someone, he will find it difficult to say, "forgive as we also have forgiven." If his heart is filled with resentment he cannot sincerely say, "Thy will be done."

Prayerful Attitudes

Our Father who art in heaven, Hallowed be Thy name.

Matthew 6:9

At the outset of his prayer Jesus acknowledged the fatherhood of God. Unless one believes that God loves his creation with the same love a father has for his children, he might as well save his breath. Unless he believes that prayers will be answered, he cannot sincerely say "our Father." If he believes that the universe is fatherly, it will follow that he is being treated as a good father would treat his son. Things that seemed fearful and hateful take on a new light. He can examine his trials with a new attitude that assures him that potential values are there.

The one who approaches the Divine must realize the vast gulf that exists between the worshiper and God. Too many individuals have thought of God only as a super-man rather than as the architect and sustainer of all creation. "Hallowed be thy name" is an acknowledgement of the majesty and dignity of God. The word "hallowed" means little to us perhaps a better translation of this Greek phrase would be "Sacred to thy name," or "Reverend be thy name." The Jews placed much more emphasis upon a name than moderns do, and the names that they gave had special meaning. Furthermore, a son could disgrace his father's name by unrighteous living. The best way in which the son could hallow the name of his father was to become a fine character himself, which would not only mean that the worshiper acknowledged the majesty of God, but that he also promised a consecration of his own life as well in order that he might honor the Father's name.

Thy Kingdom come, Thy will be done, On earth as it is in heaven.

Matthew 6:10

It is not easy to accept God's will, even when it is known. To pray that his will be done when it is unknown demands a firm

uith in the fatherly love of God. To pray this sincerely demands
hat one be able to believe that "in everything God works for
;ood with those who love him" (Romans 8:28).

A person who feels that everything is working against him, that
he world has given him the poor end of the bargain and that he
s doomed to failure cannot pray this part of the Lord's prayer
sincerely. Furthermore, a man who feels that the forces of the
universe are working against him is a person who is doomed to
unhappiness. It was the spirit of Christ to accept God's will even
when it involved the pain of the cross. At Gethsemane Jesus
found his own will opposed to what he knew to be the will of
God. Through prayer he gained the strength to accept God's will
and to face the demands that were to be made upon him.

It is the same confidence in the fatherliness of God that enables
one to pray the next part of this prayer.

Give us this day our daily bread.

Matthew 6:11

When most people desire luxuries, pleasures and wealth; when
most prayers usually include requests for more blessings, this part
of the Lord's prayer may seem trivial. But one who knows Jesus
will begin to understand that the term "bread" does not just include physical needs. "Every word that proceeds out of the mouth
of God" is mentioned as being more important than mere physical
bread. "Give us this day our daily bread" must be a request for
knowledge of spiritual things as well as for physical food.

A Bible school teacher with a half dozen pupils under his
charge has a weight of reponsibility on his shoulders that would
tax the spiritual wealth of a prophet. Only a person who is thoughtless and spiritually anemic would assume a responsibility as
heavy as this without asking for spiritual "bread" with which to
feed his soul.

Who prays for bread? The wealthy do not for they have all the
bread they want; they feel no need to pray for it. The poor in
spirit, however, who acknowledge their need for spiritual things
can sincerely pray for their daily bread. It is significant that it
was the poor in spirit whom Jesus said would gain the kingdom
of heaven. Perhaps this is one way that suffering builds spiritual
strength; those who suffer become aware of their own spiritual
poverty and then they truly can pray for bread. One of the greatest
handicaps the church has to meet is the lack of poverty of spirit
among church members.

It is at once evident how this attitude of heart banishes fear. The person who can look upon trials and persecution as potential sources of strength will no longer fear them. With this attitude of heart one has replaced a destructive attitude with a constructive one. No one can doubt that the person who can turn persecution and trial into a source of great blessings has a strength of character that will carry him through the storm. When one can turn a defeat into victory he has received an abundant answer to his prayer for daily bread.

The Christian who interprets "daily bread" only as material success is making a tragic mistake. What if a Christian businessman goes bankrupt? What if he loses everything he has? Does this mean that his prayer for daily bread has gone unanswered? Not at all, for the individual who truly believes that in everything God works for good will gain strength in what may seem to others a source of discouragement. This person has found a great source of strength which will assure him of bread every day of his life.

And forgive us our debts, As we also have forgiven our debtors;
Matthew 6:12

Further in his sermon, Jesus supplied an amplification of the meaning of this verse when he said: "For if you forgive men their trespasses, your heavenly Father also will forgive you; but if you do not forgive men their trespasses, neither will your Father forgive your trespasses" (Matt. 6:14, 15). A man may be satisfied with himself until he comes to a close study of the teachings of Jesus. Then he can see the shallowness of his spirituality and his many shortcomings which will motivate him to pray with sincerity, "forgive us our debts."

Asking God to forgive is not a request for a mere cancellation of sins, but is a plea for regeneration to spiritual power. But the man who cannot forgive others will never receive this power. The person who carries a grudge and harbors malice in his heart is an individual with a shriveled and warped attitude. Not only will he remain unforgiven, he will never achieve the spiritual maturity that comes through learning to forgive others.

The attitude of forgiveness is also a characteristic of fatherly love. What father is there who will refuse to forgive his son? A father who turns his back upon the pleas of his child and who disinherits him in spite of his pleas for forgiveness is looked upon as an evil man. The attitude of the father of the prodigal son is a perfect example of a father's willingness to forgive. If a person cannot forgive others, he is far from becoming "perfect" as our Father in heaven is perfect (Matt. 5:48).

And lead us not into temptation, but deliver us from evil.
Matthew 6:13

In the teachings of Jesus, two kinds of temptations are mentioned. The first is the temptation to use one's abilities for the wrong purposes. This is illustrated by the three temptations of Jesus in the wilderness. The second kind of temptation is to become discouraged or frightened into giving up one's mission in life. This is exemplified in Jesus' prayer in the garden of Gethsemane and in his admonition to the disciples to watch and pray lest they enter into temptation.

Those who succumb to the first temptation let their natural abilities rule in their lives in such a way that they are not devoted to Christ. Each individual has a debt to use all his talents in service to the Master. When he fails to do this he needs forgiveness, for he has failed in his major purpose in life—serving God.

How can one meet these temptations? By gaining strength through the adoption of the right spiritual attitudes. One who will be led by the teachings of Jesus to believe that God's fatherly love will prevail can approach situations armed with the strength to overcome them. Many dangers seem terrifying until one thinks of the fatherly love of God. Evil seems so attractive and the power of evil appears invincible. But the Christian can gain strength through the affirmation of his confidence in the power and might of God: "For Thine is the kingdom and the power and the glory forever."

One who truly believes that "the earth is God's and the fulness thereof" will never need to be afraid of any situation. He can realize, with comfort, that with Christ he is "more than conqueror," and that "neither death, nor life, nor angels, nor principalities, nor things present, nor things to come, nor powers, nor height, nor depth, nor anything else in all creation will be able to separate us from the love of God in Christ Jesus our Lord" (Rom. 8:38, 39).

Questions

1. Discuss some of the motivations for prayer. Which of these was the prime motive of the Pharisees?
2. Did Jesus intend his model prayer to be repeated word by word by his disciples as a liturgical formula?

3. Can a person who does not believe in the Providence of God sincerely pray "Our Father who art in heaven"?

4. What does the word "hallowed" mean? How can a son hallow the name of his father?

5. What is included in the prayer for "daily bread"? Should this be limited to physical bread?

6. What attitude of heart is necessary if one is to pray for bread?

7. How can the attitude which allows one to pray for daily bread banish fear from the life of a Christian?

8. If a Christian loses his material prosperity, must he think that his prayer for daily bread went unanswered?

9. What is included in the request for forgiveness of sins?

10. What kind of debts might we have to forgive in others?

11. What two kinds of temptations are mentioned in the teachings of Jesus? Give examples of these from the life of Jesus. Give some additional examples from modern settings.

12. How can a Christian meet and overcome temptations?

Chapter 9

The Turmoil of Fear

FEAR IS ONE of man's greatest enemies. Students of the human mind insist that even anger, with its devastating effect upon personality, does not make its victims as unhappy as fear does. Men suffer from real and imaginary fears which may be either conscious or unconscious. The fears of mankind are so numerous that it would be impossible to make a complete catalog of them. It is obvious that a person cannot be happy if his life is filled with fear. The abundant life must be one free from fear.

It is important to notice that nowhere in the teachings of Jesus can one find fear used as a motivation for being good. Jesus, unlike many modern preachers, did not use the threat of eternal punishment to force people to be good. To be sure, he made it plain that there are two alternatives facing men and that their eternal destiny depends upon which of these alternatives they choose. In no uncertain terms Jesus described the place of outer darkness where there will be weeping and gnashing of teeth, but he did not threaten his disciples with punishment if they refused to follow him. Rather, he taught that men must be motivated to serve him out of love for his kingdom. To serve him for any other reason is idolatry. Where there is this kind of love for Christ, there will be no room for fear. As the apostle John insisted, "perfect love casts out fear" (1 John 4:18).

The Problem

Part of Jesus' formula for happiness consists in a solution to the problem of fear. In the era in which Jesus lived, as in today's world, two of the chief sources of fear were love of money and fear of poverty. These two attitudes are really just two sides of the same coin, for when a person loves money it is because of an unconscious fear of insecurity and poverty. Many of the serious problems of twentieth century society are due to this fear of insecurity.

Workers fear losing their jobs or of not getting their share of the profits of the company. Managers fear bankruptcy. Marriage counselors reveal that many marriages end in turmoil because of financial troubles. Many individuals are unhappy because they have not advanced as rapidly as they had hoped and are not making as large a salary as they think they deserve. Paul was right when he observed that the love of money is the root of all kinds of evil (1 Timothy 6:10). It is not surprising that Jesus began his teachings about fear with a statement concerning wealth.

> Do not lay up for yourselves treasures on earth where moth and rust consume and where thieves break in and steal, but lay up for yourselves treasures in heaven, where neither moth nor rust consumes and where thieves do not break in and steal. For where your treasure is, there your heart will be also.
>
> Matthew 6:19-21

Although Jesus addressed an audience composed largely of poor men, he emphasized the dangers of wealth. The reason for this is that money can be just as great a peril to the poor as to the rich. Jesus did not condemn wealth just for the sake of condemning, nor did he teach that riches were evil in themselves. A close examination of his teaching will reveal that Jesus condemned money only when it became a dominating purpose in one's life.

A case in point is the rich young ruler (Matt. 19:16-22). He came to Jesus expecting to be commended for his piety. Instead, he received a difficult command, "If you would be perfect, go, sell what you possess and give to the poor, and you will have treasure in heaven; and come, follow me" (Matt. 19:21). Wealth had become a dominating factor in the life of this young man. He believed that Jesus had the secret of salvation, but his faith in money was so great and his fear of poverty so deep that he could not follow Jesus' advice. Matthew concludes his account with the words, "When the young man heard this he went away sorrowful; for he had great possessions."

Notice, however, that Jesus did not appeal to shame and guilt. Instead, he pointed out a higher level of achievement for this person. This young man had kept the commandments, but he had not mastered his fear of poverty. Instead of being concerned about permanent and abiding values, he placed all his emphasis upon perishable things. His treasure was of earth, not of heaven. He was proud of his piety, but Jesus was quick to discourage false pride and conceit, especially when men began to think too highly of themselves. But in no case did he appeal to shame.

Like so many individuals today, this young man attached tremendous value to wealth. For him it came to have security value. Jesus did not teach that wealth in itself is evil, but that the attitudes that so often accompany wealth are evil. It is not money, but the emotional attitude attached to money, that determines its effect upon one's spiritual life. Jesus did not say that it was impossible to acquire wealth and be a Christian. In fact, he says clearly that is is possible—but it is difficult. "It is easier for a camel to go through the eye of a needle than for a rich man to enter the kingdom of God." Jesus added, "With men this is impossible, but with God all things are possible" (Matt. 19:24, 26). It is possible for a rich man to be saved only when he places his wealth in its proper perspective. If he trusts in it for security, if it becomes the dominating purpose of his life, and if he fears poverty to such an extent that he refuses to use his wealth for good, his money has become an idol for him.

It is in connection with one's attitude toward money that Jesus added:

> The eye is the lamp of the body. So, if your eye is sound, your whole body will be full of light; but if your eye is not sound, your whole body will be full of darkness. If then the light in you is darkness, how great is the darkness.
>
> Matthew 6:22, 23

The older translations render this verse using the terms "single eye" and "evil eye." These were Jewish figures of speech which were understood perfectly by Jesus' audience. The "single eye" referred to bodily soundness and an attitude of liberality. The one with a "single eye," or a healthy eye, is one who has no disease and who is liberal in his giving, for he can see the need for charity and gives liberally. The "evil eye," on the other hand, refers to bodily disease and an attitude of stinginess. A man with a diseased eye cannot see the needs of others and therefore does not give to them.

Jesus is insisting that the person who is stingy and miserly, not using his wealth for proper purposes, is a blind person. But how can one develop the proper spiritual eyesight? By cultivating the quality of fatherly love. It is a physiological fact that one's eyes see what that person is looking for. Everyone has had the experience of walking down a familiar street and suddenly seeing for the first time a building that has been there for years. A husband who forgets to compliment a wife's new dress knows how easy it is to look and yet not see.

A person who has fatherly love in his heart for others will look for opportunities to use his wealth for good. The parable of the good Samaritan is an example of this. The priest and the Levite passed by the same road the Samaritan traveled. All three men looked at the same situation: a man was beaten and naked, lying by the side of the road. The priest and the Levite did not see a chance for mercy; the Samaritan did. Here is a perfect contrast between the "single eye" and the "evil eye."

This point is re-enforced by Jesus when he said:

> No one can serve two masters; for either he will hate the one and love the other, or he will be devoted to the one and despise the other. You cannot serve God and mammon.
>
> Matthew 6:24

The word which is translated here as "serve" literally means "to serve as a slave." Jesus is saying that it is impossible to dedicate one's life to two masters, although many individuals try to do just that.

The word "mammon" is untranslated, but it seems to personify wealth. Jesus was not saying, as some have supposed, "you cannot be faithful to God and have riches," but rather, "you cannot be faithful to God and make an idol of riches." The reason for not laying up treasures on earth is that it involves a divided allegiance. The man who trusts in wealth will be unable to trust wholly in Christ. To attempt to lay up treasures in heaven and on earth at the same time is a spiritual impossibility, comparable to the physical impossibility of trying to jump up and down at the same instant.

The Cure

Jesus was not one to leave his listeners without a firm plan for future activity. Jesus not only described the ailment, he also prescribed the cure.

> Therefore I tell you, do not be anxious about your life, what you shall eat or what you shall drink, nor about your body, what you shall put on. Is not life more than food, and the body more than clothing? Look at the birds of the air: they neither sow nor reap nor gather into barns, and yet your heavenly Father feeds them. Are you not of more value than they? And which of you by being anxious can add one cubit to his span of life? And why are you anxious about clothing? Consider the lilies of the field, how they grow; they neither toil nor spin; yet I tell you, even Solomon in

all his glory was not arrayed like one of these. But if God so clothed the grass of the field, which today is alive and tomorrow is thrown into the oven, will he not much more clothe you, O men of little faith? Therefore do not be anxious, saying, 'What shall we eat?' or 'What shall we drink?' or 'What shall we wear?' For the Gentiles seek all these things; and your heavenly Father knows that you need them all. But seek first his kingdom and his righteousness, and all these things shall be yours as well."

Therefore, do not be anxious about tomorrow, for tomorrow will be anxious for itself. Let the day's own trouble be sufficient for the day.

Matthew 6:25-34

Many individuals misunderstand the meaning of this passage, for on first reading it sounds as if it were a plea for irresponsibility and shortsightedness. It appears as a dreamy but impractical piece of poetry, valuable for its idealistic goals, but utterly impractical for everyday living. Part of the blame for this lies in the older translations of this passage which rendered the first part of verse 25 as "take no thought." The Greek phrase in question here is better translated as "do not be anxious" as the revised version words it. Anxiety is the key thought of the passage. "Be not afraid about tomorrow, about food or raiment." The passage is not a plea for irresponsibility, but for faith.

Jesus comments upon the futility of anxiety when he said, "And which of you by being anxious can add one cubit to his span of life?" Jesus points out in an almost humorous way that worry and anxiety rarely change a situation. The word "span of life" could also be translated "stature." The truth of what Jesus is saying is that a person can add neither height to his stature nor years to his life through anxiety. In fact, modern studies have shown that a person actually decreases his chances for longevity by needless worry, anxiety and fear.

Whenever a person becomes afraid, his whole body reacts in such a way as to summon all his physical strength to meet an impending challenge. His body is prepared for self protection or to make him able to run as rapidly as possible. Adrenalin pours into the system. Digestive processes cease. Blood from the head and stomach rushes to the arms and legs; the heart beats faster to provide more energy for strenuous activity. Blood sugar is secreted in greater quantities into the blood stream with the result that the muscles are stronger than normal.

These reactions would be invaluable in a civilization where physical combat was called for. But in modern society the usual effect is to produce indigestion, because the digestive processes have ceased to function, and to decrease resistance to disease, because the unused fuel thrown into the muscles has to be carried off or it is left there where it is not needed. The resistance mechanisms of the body have to waste their energy in scavenger service, and leave the body less protected from disease. Fear certainly does not add to the length of one's life.

Many individuals believe they can overcome their fears and anxieties by will power alone, but this is not true. Fear cannot be attacked as an abstract force any more than love can be mastered by a simple wish to love everybody. Jesus did not treat fear as a generality, but rather dealt with special fear attitudes—namely, those that arise from too much faith in money, food and clothing. These are the things which play the greatest part in everyday living. But, if a person places his trust in some other power than these things, he will have gone a long way toward overcoming his fears.

Knowledge is the first key to dispelling fear. When a person realizes that life is more than riches, food or clothing, these material things seem less important. Physical accessories have become so much a part of life that many individuals possess a deep seated fear of being without them. Yet Jesus asked, "Is not life more than food, and the body more than clothing?" Men often fear things for no better reason than that they have always feared them. To realize that their fears are groundless is a great help in overcoming them.

A second attitude which provides a key to overcoming fear is trust. A child may be afraid, but if he can place his hand in his father's, his fear disappears. The conviction that the universe is fatherly will remove the reason for many fears that possess individuals. To depend upon God even when one does not understand the reason why is a prerequisite for overcoming the destructive power of fear.

A third attitude necessary for overcoming fear is to have a dominating purpose in life. A man who has a goal and wants to achieve that goal more than anything else in the world will not be alarmed by situations which would frighten others less determined than he. Many young men have obtained a college education in spite of almost impossible odds. Rather than worry about how to pay tuition, how to buy books, or where the next meal was coming from, they devoted themselves to the task of getting an education. They happily discovered that their other problems seemed less formidable. The purpose which Jesus suggests is: "Seek first his kingdom and his righteousness, and all these things shall be yours as well." The individual who is concerned about the salvation of souls will have little time for anxiety and fear.

Questions

1. Did Jesus use fear as a motivation for morality? Cite examples from his personal ministry when he could have used fear to prompt obedience and did not. For example, see John 6:66-69.
2. What is the significance of John's statement, "perfect love casts out fear"?
3. How are the fear of poverty and the love of money similar?
4. In what sense is money the root of all evil? (1 Timothy 6:10)
5. Why did Jesus preach on the dangers of wealth even though his audience was largely composed of poor men?
6. What emotional attitudes that are often attached to money make it idolatrous? What attitudes toward money will keep one out of the kingdom of heaven?
7. Why is fatherly love necessary for the proper use of wealth? Give examples showing how fatherly love uses money.
8. What is the key thought of Matthew 6:25-34? Give reasons to support the conviction that this is not a plea for irresponsibility but for faith?
9. How can one overcome fear and anxiety? Can the problem be attacked in a general way?
10. What are three attitudes necessary for dispelling fear?
11. What makes fear incompatible with the abundant life?

Chapter 10

The Turmoil of Anger

"WHOEVER IS ANGRY is in for trouble!" This one sentence summary perfectly expresses the crux of Jesus' teaching about anger. The Lord made it clear that the person who expects to be happy must master his anger.

Jesus placed more emphasis upon fear and anger than he did upon any other human emotions. He illustrated, by example after example, the attitudes one should cultivate to conquer anger. The old saying, "The measure of a man is the size of the thing it takes to get his goat" contains a large measure of truth. The number of things that cause anger in a man are inversely proportional to his greatness. "Standing up for one's rights" and insisting on "the principle of the thing" makes a person seem pretty small next to the individual who can overcome evil with good.

There may be times when one should become angry, just as there are times when strychnine is a valuable medicine. But a person cannot make a steady diet out of either strychnine or anger. A man whose life is ruled by anger will never find true happiness. No wonder Jesus had so much to say about anger.

> You have heard that it was said to the men of old, 'You shall not kill; and whoever kills shall be liable to judement.' But I say to you that everyone who is angry with his brother shall be liable to judgment; whoever insults his brother shall be liable to council, and whoever says, 'You fool!' shall be liable to the hell of fire.
> Matthew 5:21, 22

Laws against murder have been in existence for thousands of years, yet murder still continues. Jesus makes plain that murder is the symptom; anger is the cause. If a person is to prevent murder, he must first conquest anger and hate. Perhaps one could paraphrase this teaching by recasting it into the form of another of Jesus' teachings and say, "He who looks upon his brother in anger and desires to kill him has committed murder already in his heart."

In the passage just quoted, Jesus gives the anatomy of murder. A person first becomes angry with his brother; then he utters, "raca," probably a statement of contempt. His anger increases to the point that he lashes out at his brother with the words, "You fool," a statement which carried a worse connotation to the Jews than it does today. It was as insulting a term as a person could use. All these actions are steps on the road to murder. If one would effectively stop murder, he must get to the root of the problem. In his characteristic manner, Jesus concentrated on the attitudes of heart which cause murder rather than an outward behavior.

The effect of anger on the body is similar to the effect of fear. Whenever a person becomes angry, his body prepares itself as rapidly as possible for physical struggle. It calls a halt to any unnecessary bodily processes, one of which is digestion. Sugar is secreted into the blood stream giving additional fuel to be burned as energy. The heart begins working faster to increase the blood supply; blood is rushed to the muscles of the arms and legs. In such a state a person is physically stronger and is prepared to fight. But usually in modern society he does not fight. He only grips the steering wheel a little tighter, clamps down on the accelerator a little harder, grinds his teeth a couple of times and drives on, thinking only of what he would like to do to the other driver. Not only is his food undigested, but the excess sugar in his blood has to be carried off as waste matter. The inner tension left by a fit of anger is testimony to the damaging effect it has upon the human body. It is more than a figure of speech to say that anger is poisonous.

To conquer anger one must do more than merely try to change outward actions. A person may seem calm on the surface, although underneath a still facade there is a raging sea of emotion. Trying to cure the problem by attacking the symptom is about as effective as trying to cure measles by cutting out the spots. He must get at the source of the trouble—anger. He must try to turn those situations that cause anger into situations that arouse some other emotion within him. In short, he must replace anger and fear with love and faith. In the next passage Jesus strikes at the heart of the problem when he urges his followers to overcome anger with love.

> So if you are offering your gift at the altar, and there remember that your brother has something against you, leave your gift there before the altar and go; first be reconciled to your brother, and then come and offer your gift.
>
> Matthew 5:23, 24

If "your brother has something against you." There is no thought of whether it is justly or unjustly. Nor did Jesus say, "If you have something against your brother," but rather, if your brother has anger in his heart toward you. The small man is likely to return the anger of his brother with anger. But Jesus preaches a righteousness which goes beyond the righteousness of the scribes and Pharisees. He indicates that the way to solve social problems is not to meet half way, for there is always disagreement as to where the halfway mark if located. Rather, one should be willing to go all the way, if that is what it takes to destroy the anger in another's heart.

"If you are offering your gift at the altar." The place of animal sacrifice is no longer a part of God's revealed will. But there is a modern application. Many individuals come weekly to the Lord's Supper without the slightest preparation of this sort. Jesus might say today that no Christian should come to the Communion table until he has prepared himself by offering love to someone who hates him. The Lord's Supper commemorates the fact that the Savior gave his life for those who hated him and were angry at him; should a Christian not be able to forgive at least one brother? If every Christian, before each Lord's Supper, became reconciled with one brother who held hate against him, what a powerful influence the church would have.

But so often individuals defend their actions by saying that their anger was prompted by "righteous indignation," a term which has been the cover for a multitude of sins. Righteous indignation was not unknown to Jesus; in fact, he used it at times. He also left an example of how it should be expressed. Perhaps the most beautiful example of his method of showing righteous indignation was at the Last Supper. It was customary to provide guests with a towel and a basin of water, and if the host were wealthy, with a servant to wash their feet. Men went barefoot or wore sandals, and at the end of a long day their feet would be dusty and tired.

At the last Supper the disciples were bickering as to who among them would be the greatest in the kingdom. Probably, each scrupulously avoided the bathing materials. It was here that Jesus showed the right way to express righteous indignation. He washed their feet himself. Probably no group of men were more completely ashamed or rebuked than were his disciples. No angry words could have been so effective in making them realize the pettiness of their attitudes. Yet Jesus did it in a spirit of perfect love. There were no angry words. No frayed tempers. None of the disciples failed to feel the sting of its rebuke or the healing power of the love which prompted it.

Jesus' principle is to overcome evil with good. His practical application of this principle at first seems astonishing.

> Make friends quickly with your accuser, while you are going with him to court, lest your accuser hand you over to the judge, and the judge to the guard, and you be put in prison; truly, I say to you, you will never get out till you have paid the last penny.
>
> Matthew 5:25, 26

The picture painted here by Jesus describes a scene common to his day. It was the custom of the courts then to cause the defendant and the plantiff to walk into court together. The hope was that they might settle their differences on the way and save the trouble of a trial. The plan did not work too well, however, for usually both walked into court with an air of complete disdain for the other, looking like two angry playmates.

Sources of Anger

Students of the human mind insist that there are really only three basic causes for anger: (1) wounded vanity—having others think less of us than we think we deserve; (2) real or imagined injustice to ourselves or our friends; and (3) blocked behavior—being prevented from doing what we want to do. Jesus deals with all three types of attitudes in the succeeding verses.

The first cause of anger, wounded vanity, is illustrated in the attitudes of the two men on the way to court. Neither will take the first step toward reconciliation, for he doubtless feels that this would be surrender on his part. Yet Jesus said, "Make friends quickly with your accuser." This may seem to involve a loss of dignity, but anger is hardly a better alternative. The truth of the matter is that in spite of a person's claim to righteous indignation, he becomes most angry when he is in the wrong. Most individuals are much more angered by just than by unjust criticism.

The word which is translated "agree" carries a much deeper meaning than is usually indicated by the English word. It literally means to "be in good mind," or "to be well inclined toward." Jesus is not recommending cowardice, but love. When one remains angry it matters little whether he won or lost the case. It is lost anyway.

Another of the causes for anger is real or imagined injustice. It is with this attitude that Jesus deals next:

> You have heard that it was said, 'An eye for an eye and a tooth for a tooth.' But I say to you, Do not resist one who is evil. But

if anyone strikes you on the right cheek, turn to him the other also.

> Matthew 5:38, 39

"An eye for an eye and a tooth for a tooth" has come to have an undesirable meaning. But when this principle was given it was a great improvement over the ethics of its day, for "a life for an eye and a head for a tooth" was more in keeping with the prevailing moral codes. As long as anger is the dominating motive of behavior, ethics such as this are likely to prevail. Watch two boys in a fist fight. Each tries to make his blow a little harder than the last. Anger is like that. It wants a "life for an eye and a head for a tooth."

Rather than return anger for anger, Jesus urges his followers to return love for hate, even though it is costly to do so. The situation Jesus described is an interesting one. If one were being attacked, his assailant would probably use his right hand and strike him on the left cheek. But Jesus said, "If anyone strikes you on the right cheek." If a person were insulting another individual, he would slap him with the back of his right hand, as was the custom in that day, so striking him on the right cheek. It is probable that Jesus is here describing such a blow.

Notice that Jesus did not say that one will not be struck if he turns the left cheek. What he is saying is that the only way to overcome injustice is with love. Many individuals have the mistaken idea that "passive resistance" is the ideal that Jesus is teaching here. They seem to make the assumption that if one is not resisting with force, he is not resisting. But this is not what Jesus taught, for he insisted that the only way to overcome evil is with love. Those who stage sit-in and sit-down demonstrations are generally motivated by hatred of their oppressor and have anger in their hearts because of the injustice they are demonstrating against.

In the next verses Jesus applies this principle to other characteristic situations.

> and if any one would sue you and take your coat, let him have your cloak as well; and if any one forces you to go one mile, go with him two miles. Give to him who begs from you, and do not refuse him who would borrow from you.
>
> Matthew 5:40-42

In Jesus' day, the Roman occupation troops had the right to force any citizen to run any kind of errand or to render any service that was deemed needed. This made the Jews furious. To be forced to do anything by a hated Roman soldier was more than they could bear!

This brings up the third cause of anger—blocked behavior. Whenever a person wants to do something and is prevented from doing it by somebody else, he becomes angry. Jesus taught that the way to keep from being angry is to overcome the situation with love. Do more than you are forced to, and you will have won the battle.

"Give to him who begs from you, and do not refuse him who would borrow from you." Perhaps few pests are as distasteful as the chronic borrower. The usual reaction is to turn a person like this away in anger, refusing to lend him anything. The effect of this action is to create anger both in the heart of the lender and the borrower. Jesus was probably not saying that one should meet the request and lend exactly what was requested. He does not say that. He does say that the borrower must not be turned away in anger.

Consider the principle of fatherly love. When a child comes to a loving father to make a request, the father listens carefully and patiently. He may not grant the request, for the child's welfare may demand that he refuse. But he does not send the child away in anger.

The verb that is here translated "refuse" has a strong meaning. It includes the idea of "drive away," or "to turn to flight." A loving father would not drive his child away when the child comes to him with a request. In a similar way, one should not drive away a borrower with a fit of anger, but rather should try to use the situation to exhibit an attitude of love. This is not always the easy way, but it is the better way; better for him that asks and for him that grants the request.

In his concluding statement on anger, Jesus offered a new set of attitudes.

> You have heard that it was said, 'You shall love your neighbor and hate your enemy.' But I say to you, Love your enemies, and pray for those who persecute you, so that you may be sons of your Father who is in heaven; for he makes his sun rise on the evil and on the good, and sends rain on the just and on the unjust. For if you love those who love you, what reward have you? Do not even the tax collectors do the same? And if you salute only your brethren, what more are you doing than others? Do not even the Gentiles do the same?
>
> Matthew 5:43-47

"Love your enemies" has been called the impossible commandment. Yet Jesus pointed out an amazing insight. Even the most degraded and perverse individuals love their own friends. If a Christian would be like his Father in heaven, he certainly must do more than others. Loving one's enemies is the Christian ideal. It may not be easy, but it is right. The word translated "enemy" does not refer to enemies in war or mortal enemies. It really means "hated one." In other words, Jesus says, "Love those whom you hate."

One frequently is told that he must love his enemies while hating the things that they do. Love the sinner but not the sin. C. S. Lewis remarks: "For a long time I used to think this a silly, straw-splitting distinction: how could you hate what a man did and not hate the man? But years later it occurred to me that there was one man to whom I had been doing this all my life —namely myself."

This, then, is Jesus' formula for happiness. Return good for evil. Overcome evil with good. These are steps on the road to becoming "perfect, as your heavenly Father is perfect" (Matt. 5:48).

Questions

1. What are some attitudes that are motivated by anger?
2. What is there about anger that makes it incompatible with the abundant life?
3. What is the effect of anger on the human body? Is this a good or bad effect?
4. Can one conquer anger by merely working on the outward manifestations of it? Discuss this thoroughly in connection with the teachings of this part of the sermon on the mount.
5. Is it a Christian principle to meet an estranged brother half-way? Will this attitude overcome hate and anger?
6. Is righteous indignation ever justified?
7. What is righteous indignation? How did the practice of righteous indignation in the life of Jesus differ from the way many individuals seek to use it?
8. Why did Jesus urge his followers to make reconciliation with their adversaries quickly? Is it harder to be reconciled the longer one waits?
9. What are the three basic sources of anger?
10. Discuss the principle "An eye for an eye and a tooth for a tooth." When it was given, was it an undesirable standard of conduct?
11. How is it possible for one to love his enemy? What did Jesus have in mind when he commanded this? Who is your enemy?

Chapter 11

Inferiority Feelings

DID YOU EVER wonder why some individuals are so sensitive and why others are so conceited? Curiously enough, both reactions serve the same purpose. Here are a few of the other attitudes which have a similar origin: vanity, jealousy, envy, anxiety, always having hard luck, bullying, gossip, inability to take criticism, pretending to know it all, refusing to join groups, extreme desire for flattery, grandstand playing, being a poor loser, extreme profanity, pugnacity, suspiciousness, and many others. Most of the time the reason, or one of the reasons, for this kind of behavior is a feeling of inferiority.

Everybody wants to be successful. This is just as normal as man's desire for food. Because of a realization that complete success is impossible, many individuals feel inferior. Every person feels inferior to some degree, although the ways this feeling expresses itself are as varied as the individuals themselves. In the seventh chapter of Matthew, Jesus gives some teachings which have a remarkable application to this problem. He shows how one can overcome his feeling of inferiority and how he can find happiness instead of anxiety.

This is not to say that this application of the teachings of this chapter will exhaust their meaning. Obviously, such things as the golden rule have a much wider application than will be explored here. The point is that if one masters these teachings of Jesus, he will discover that there is no room in his personailty for feelings of inferiority.

Men who have studied human behavior reveal a curious thing about feelings of inferiority. They have discovered that the individual who has some weakness usually tried to hide this fact by being very sensitive about it and emphasizing its opposite characteristic. This attitude is called compensation. For example, a short individual may try to compensate for the feeling of inferiority his stature gives him by being loud and boistrous in the presence of others. He will be easily insulted by any reference to his height.

Do Not Judge

In the first few passages of the seventh chapter of Matthew, Jesus discusses some of the abnormal activities that are common forms of compensation for feelings of inferiority.

> Judge not, that you be not judged. For with the judgment you pronounced you will be judged, and the measure you give will be the measure you get.
>
> Matthew 7:1, 2

The word that is here translated "judge" literally means "judge adversely." Jesus is saying, "Do not always look for the worst in men."

One of the most insidious and abnormal compensations for feelings of inferiority is gossip. There are really two ways a person can gain a higher opinion of himself. The first of these is to increase his estimate of himself by personal achievement. The other is to lower his estimate of his neighbor, which is expressed in an effort to make others think less of his neighbor. By pushing his neighbor down, he unconsciously feels that he has lifted himself up. This is the aim of gossip. The one who gossips is rarely interested in harming his neighbor; he is concerned about helping himself. Notice that gossips seldom talk about persons in a lower social scale. Gossip is usually restricted to those within the same social circle.

Another interesting characteristic of gossip is that it usually focuses attention upon characteristics of which the gossiper himself is guilty. Those who have studied human behavior call this projection. Simply stated this means a tendency to judge others by oneself. For example, the dishonest man is invariably suspicious of the honesty of others. The liar never believes anybody else.

What are the results of this kind of compensation for feelings of inferiority? Failure. Nobody likes to be around an individual who is conceited, haughty, sensitive, or who possesses any of the other attitudes caused by inferiority feelings. The person who tries to increase his own estimation in the eyes of others by gossiping is using a hopeless type of compensation, for it implies that he has no hope of building himself up. He only hopes to bring others down to his level.

Another way to compensate for feelings of inferiority closely akin to gossip is that of drawing attention away from oneself by becoming critical of others. Concerning this attitude Jesus said:

> Why do you seek the speck that is in your brother's eye, but do not notice the log that is in your own eye? Or how can you say to your brother, 'Let me take the speck out of your eye,' when there is the log in your own eye? You hypocrite, first take the log out of your own eye, and then you will see clearly to take the speck out of your brother's eye.
>
> Matthew 7:3-5

Here again, Jesus uses some of his characteristic humor. A man with a telephone pole hanging out of his eye tries to remove a speck from the eye of his neighbor. Can one imagine a more pitiable sight than this? Yet this is exactly the kind of spectacle many persons present.

When an individual's inferiority feelings are prompted by a lack of moral stamina, he is ashamed of his sinfulness and becomes anxious that it will not be seen. He attempts to hide his own faults by pointing to the fact that others are as sinful as he. He does this by picking flaws in the character of others. Unlike the gossip, who tries to pull the other fellow down to his own livel, this individual tries to gain a feeling of superiority by seeming to help the other person. He thus directs attention away from his own beams to the other person's motes.

When this tendency has progressed to its extreme forms, the result is the Elmer Gantry type of person—the man who becomes a fanatic in order to hide some glaring fault in his own life. This is exemplified by the businessman who spearheads a campaign to oust mixed swimming in the public schools while at the same time he cheats his business associates out of thousands of dollars. This is sometimes the reason preachers get "hobbies." By focusing their attention upon some detail of doctrine, they are able to divert attention from a real problem in their own character.

Jesus' advice to such a person is to first get rid of the beam. Try to see things in their proper perspective. Again, in his characteristic way, Jesus attacks the root of the problem. He does not condemn the external actions but rather urges a reformation of attitude. If a person will first rid his life of faults, he will have destroyed the reason for gossip and fault finding. If he recognizes his own inabilities and short comings, faces them squarely and tries to overcome them, he will have no need for pulling others down to his level through gossip. If he exerts his energy in destroying the beam in his own eye, he will not be compelled to pick the flaws in the personalities of others.

Pearls Before Swine

> Do not give dogs what is holy; and do not throw your pearls before swine, lest they trample them underfoot and turn to attack you.
>
> Matthew 7:6

There is a third way that individuals seek to compensate for feelings of inferiority. This is an excessive quest for popularity. A young man who has so little confidence in his ability to make friends that he "joins the crowd" is an example of casting one's pearls before swine. The young girl who accepts the notion that unless she deserts her ideals she will not be popular soon discovers that the swine have turned on her. Instead of finding popularity, she discovers her ideals trampled on, herself discarded, and an opportunity lost to help one man evolve from swinehood to manhood.

Everybody wants to be liked. This is especially true among young people who acutely feel the need for popularity. Too often young people are willing to throw their ideals to the swine in an effort to be popular. Thinking this is a good investment, they soon discover that popularity is fickle and may change at a moment's notice.

Another reaction caused by feelings of inferiority are the attitudes of fatalism and pessimism. The student who fails a class finds it much more convenient to blame it on the teacher rather than upon his own laziness. The businessman who goes bankrupt consoles himself by insisting that his failure was not really his fault, but was because the forces of fate were against him. It is with these attitudes in mind that Jesus said:

> Ask, and it will be given you; seek, and you will find; knock, and it will be opened to you. For everyone who asks receives, and he who seeks finds, and to him who knocks it will be opened.
>
> Matthew 7:7, 8

No Christian who believes in the power of God can very well have feelings of inferiority and pessimism. If a man has a strong inferiority feeling with respect to his ability to accomplish things, he lacks faith.

There is no promise that one will be given that for which he asks, or that he will find exactly what he is seeking, or that the door on which he is knocking will open. He does have the promise, however, that the answer to his petition will be good.

Or what man of you, if his son asks him for a loaf, will give him a stone? Or if he asks for a fish, will give him a serpent? If you then, who are evil, know how to give good gifts to your children, how much more will your Father who is in heaven give good things to those who ask him?

Man is essentially a dependent individual. However courageous he may be or pretend to be, he needs someone to depend upon. But if he feels that he is in the midst of a cruel and heartless universe in which there is no one upon whom he can depend, he may begin to feel insignificant and inferior. He then becomes a pessimist who insists that life is all an illusion, that actually one is quite likely to receive a "stone" when he asks for fish. Attitudes such as this are the results of feelings of inferiority.

The cure for this attitude is a simple one. Jesus points out that things which may seem to be "stones" and "serpents" in reality are not. This new attitude calls for faith, for Jesus insisted that God is the kind of Father who will give only good gifts to children. If "stones" are given instead of bread, one should search for their meaning, being sure that it is out of love that they are given. The spirit of this teaching is perfectly illustrated by a prayer written by an anonymous Confederate soldier. It is entitled *The Creed of a Soldier.*

He asked for strength that he might achieve; he was made weak that he might obey.

He asked for health that he might do greater things; he was given infirmity that he might do better things.

He asked for riches that he might be happy; he was given poverty that he might be wise.

He asked for power that he might have the praise of men; he was given weakness that he might feel the need of God.

He asked for all things that he might enjoy life; he was given life that he might enjoy all things.

He had nothing that he asked for, but everything that he hoped for.

His prayer is answered.

He is most blessed.

Concern for Others

Whenever a person does not want to be with other people, it probably is because he feels inferior. Those who withdraw from society often do so because they think that others do not want to be with them. How can a person behave toward others in an effort to overcome this dangerous attitude? Jesus' answer is well known.

So whatever you wish that men would do to you, do so to them.

Matthew 7:12

Many individuals who profess to live by this command have given it some strange interpretations. One of these is, "Do unto others as they do unto you." But this is in fundamental disagreement with Jesus' principle of overcoming evil with good. This attitude returns anger for anger and hate for hate. It never solves any problems; it only increases them.

Other professed followers of this doctrine seem to think that it says, "Do unto others as they do unto you, only do it first." Those who follow this creed are always on the defensive. If their neighbor gets a better job or a higher salary, this is evidence to them that it was obtained through unfair methods. A person with this attitude then reads evil connotations into all of his neighbor's behavior. The result is unhappiness and mental turmoil.

This teaching of Jesus is so important because it offers a cure for feelings of inferiority. In a nutshell the cure is this: replace bad habits with good ones. One who keeps busy doing things for others will find his own fears and selfishness pushed to the background. Through the achievement that comes from serving others he will find the satisfaction that comes from accomplishment. Happily, he will discover that many of his feelings of inferiority have vanished.

Jesus concludes his remarks in this section with the words:

Enter by the narrow gate; for the gate is wide and the way is easy, that leads to destruction, and those who enter by it are many. For the gate is narrow and the way is hard, that leads to life, and those who find it are few.

Matthew 7:13, 14

A final command of Jesus is to avoid the broad and easy way. It should be noticed that the phrase is "narrow and hard," not "steep and crooked" as many seem to think. It is hard to find and hard to follow. Few find it. The other way is "wide and easy," not "comfortable and appealing." The teachings of Jesus indicate that the only way to happiness lies in the acceptance of the principles he advocated. The broad way that leads to destruction is filled with miserable people—individuals who are tormented by their own pettiness and shortcomings. The narrow way, on the other hand, may be hard to find. But it alone offers life.

Questions

1. Why do many individuals feel inferior? Is this a normal or an abnormal reaction?
2. What effects might be caused by feelings of inferiority?
3. Why do some persons gossip about others? What is the motivation for gossip? What was Jesus' attitude toward it?
4. What prompts an attitude of fault finding? How does this cover up feelings of inferiority?
5. How did Jesus attack the problems of gossip and fault finding?
6. What are fanaticism and "hobby riding" symptoms of?
7. What ways do individuals seek popularity that in reality mean they are throwing their pearls before swine?
8. What is Jesus' cure for an attitude of pessimism and fatalism?
9. What was Jesus' assurance about prayer? What attitudes are necessary for acceptable prayer?
10. Is it a normal reaction for an individual to not want to associate with other people? What is this attitude a symptom of?
11. How does an application of the golden rule help cure this dangerous attitude.
12. Discuss the thirteenth and fourteenth verses of Matthew seven. Is the broad way a comfortable way? Are those on the broad way happy?

Chapter 12

The Christian Personality

THERE ARE MANY leaders seeking followers. There are many philosophies of life. Almost everyone speaks authoritatively on how life ought to be lived; how children should be reared; and how one's attitudes should be formed. How can a person distinguish between them? Science would say, "examine them." Jesus said:

> Beware of false prophets who come to you in sheep's clothing but inwardly are ravenous wolves. You will know them by their fruits.
>
> Matthew 7:15

In the final section of the Sermon on the Mount, Jesus deals with the problem of choosing a set of attitudes. Verse 15 is the first of a series of three descriptions of false prophets.

Perhaps there has never been a time when it was more important to be able to distinguish between false and true prophets. Clever advertisements make their appeal from the glossy pages of modern magazines. Quacks offer, for a price, the secrets of how to be happy; how to be well liked; and how to influence others. Christian sects have proliferated almost beyond numeration, and unbelief has never come in more sophisticated dress.

How can one distinguish between that which is true and that which is false? The first test is that false prophets come in sheep's clothing. It would be noticed that they do not come in shepherd's clothing. They do not even profess to be leaders, for sheep are followers, not leaders. These false prophets come calling themselves representatives of "common folk." They talk about "us plain common people." They insist that they are representatives of the crowd.

What is the advantage of this approach? In the first place, these false prophets do not make their appeal to human needs. The "sheep's clothing" leader appeals not to his own ability as a leader, not to his cause, but to the conceit of the people. He makes them feel that they are the leaders and he is simply one of them. The crowd is pleased at this tickling of their vanity. They flock to leaders like this in droves, for such a leader is just one of them—just plain folks.

The first criterion for spotting a wolf in sheep's clothing is the nature of his appeal. If he appeals to one's vanity, a person can be certain that this is the appeal of a false prophet. If fear, anger, hate, greed or suspicion are the sources of appeal, this too means that the advocate of these things is a wolf in sheeps clothing. This is closely akin to the second way of testing a prophet—look at the results.

> Are grapes gathered from thorns, or figs from thistles? So every sound tree bears good fruit, but the bad tree bears evil fruit. A sound tree cannot bear evil fruit, nor can a bad tree bear good fruit. Every tree that does not bear good fruit is cut down and thrown into the fire. Thus, you will know them by their fruits.
>
> Matthew 7:16-20

It is interesting to notice that orientals did not believe in raising trees just for looks. If the tree did not bear fruit, it was cut down. The corrupt tree is not necessarily a rotten tree, but a tree that is worthless. Perhaps this figure could be used to describe those individuals who are good, but not good for anything.

A prophet is to be judged by the effect of his message. If his message produces heartache, anxiety or unhappiness, it is evident that he is a false prophet. Many an individual has followed a false prophet into easy and selfish attitudes and found himself in the "fire" of unhappiness because of his unwholesome character. If the false prophets are themselves "thorns and thistles," it will inevitably be the cause that their followers will have the same characteristics. This is not to say that all false prophets are evil and insidious men. They may be perfectly sincere, but sincerity is not enough. Jesus indicated this when he asserted:

> Not everyone who says to me, 'Lord, Lord,' shall enter the kingdom of heaven, but he who does the will of my Father who is in heaven. On that day many will say to me, 'Lord, Lord, did we not prophesy in your name, and cast out demons in your name, and do many mighty works in your name?' and then I will declare to them, 'I never knew you; depart from me, you evildoers.'
>
> Matthew 7:21-23

There are individuals who imagine that salvation can be achieved by human effort. They become great public speakers, or seek good educations. They believe that good works will bring salvation. They give generously to the church and to benevolent purposes. But they all miss one thing. They reject the spiritual principles taught by Jesus. The foolishness of this attitude is illustrated by Jesus when he said:

> Everyone then who hears these words of mine and does not do them will be like a foolish man who built his house upon the sand; and the rain fell and the floods came, and the winds blew and beat against that house, and it fell, and great was the fall of it.
> Matthew 7:26-27

There is a common attitude that one can learn the principles of moral conduct and put them into effect whenever he desires. Many persons feel that they can accept the teachings of Jesus intellectually, but that these teachings are too idealistic to be put into effect. Both of these attitudes overlook the fact' that one only learns by doing. No one would expect to learn football, skating, or baseball by a correspondence course. What reason, then, is there for thinking that the teachings of Christ can be learned even if they are not put into practice? The truth is that a person who seeks to accept the teachings of Jesus intellectually but refuses to apply them in his life is building his character upon a shaky foundation.

What happens to a person who accepts but does not act upon what he has accepted? Assuming that he is convinced, that he gives intellectual assent, but that he does not act upon his convictions, what will be the result of his personality? The fact is that although he may not be acting upon the set of values he has intellectually accepted, he is acting upon some set of values. One must act on something. When he faces a situation he reacts to it in some way. His reaction may be one of fear or anger, joy, pleasure, love or a mixture of these.

There is no question of whether or not one has a system of values; it is only a question of which system of values he accepts. The man who thinks that he is a Christian but does not act on Christian principles is only fooling himself. He may act in a somewhat Christian manner when things are going well, but when the rains descend and the floods come and the winds blow, he will fall back upon some other set of values. His Christianity will reveal itself as only being surface deep.

Many individuals survive mentally only because they are fortunate enough to be sheltered from the rains and floods and winds of life. The measure of the strength of one's personality is found when the going gets rough. A man may outwardly have subscribed to the principles taught by Christ. Inwardly his god may be money and the things that money will buy. As long as this business prospers, as long as his bank account shows six figures, he is happy and contented. But let his business falter; let him lose all that he has; and his professed Christianity may be tossed to the wind. Many men want to "curse God and die" when things go wrong. This attitude reveals a life built on a sandy foundation.

It is impossible to build strong structures upon weak foundations, but it is possible to lay strong foundations.

> Everyone then who hears these words of mine and does them will be like a wise man who built his house upon the rock; and the rain fell, and the floods came, and the winds blew and beat upon that house, but it did not fall, because it had been founded on the rock.
>
> Matthew 7:24-25

One who accepts Jesus as the guiding ideal of his life and who identifies himself with Jesus by his action can hope to stand against whatever forces try to overwhelm him. To enable a child to develop a strong personality and character, parents must teach him the right attitudes by building his life on a strong foundation.

Parents must give their children the firm belief that there are great spiritual principles which, if applied, can solve the problems of life. Children should be taught that whatever happens is in accordance with these laws, and that if they will apply these principles to their lives, they can achieve great happiness for themselves and for others.

Parents should endeavor to instill within their children the conviction that the universe is fatherly. Children should be made anxious to serve the will of God, whatever this duty may demand. In short, if children are to build their lives on a firm foundation, they must be taught to conform their lives to that of Jesus. Since the only knowledge of the Savior that children have comes through parents and teachers, one can see the heavy weight of responsibility that falls on the shoulders of adults.

Parents can help their children build their lives on sound spiritual principles by finding for them opportunities for acts of mercy. Let them perform them for those whom they love. They will happily discover that they get pleasure from them. One pleasurable experience in serving others will do more toward making a child a loving personality than years of moral teaching about right and wrong in Sunday school.

MOMENTS ON THE MOUNT

And when Jesus finished these sayings, the crowds were astonished at his teaching, for he taught them as one who had authority, and not as their scribes.

Matthew 7:28, 29

The term "astonishment" carries here the connotation of "being greatly impressed," rather than that of mere amazement. They were impressed because Jesus taught them as one having an ultimate authority. His teaching appealed to the very nature of things. He reached down deeply into their hearts and provided for their innermost needs.

Can you imagine a scientist urging his students to believe in the law of gravitation because George Washington or Abraham Lincoln believed in it? He does not need to make his appeal to authority, for he is teaching laws which are explanations of the very nature of things. Jesus taught that same kind of law. He did not urge his followers to love their neighbors because they ought to, or because it was their duty, or because a number of great religious teachers had advocated the loving of neighbors. Jesus emphasized that love for neighbors—even love for enemies—was necessary for the development of strong character. "You will know them by their fruits." This was Jesus' principle of vindication. Try out these spiritual principles and see whether or not they are part of the universal plan of things. It is no wonder that Jesus' hearers were astonished.

Questions

1. What are some of the marks of false prophets?
2. How can one make a choice between conflicting loyalties? What criteria did Jesus urge upon his followers for making this kind of choice?
3. Is sincerity a sufficient guide in choosing a set of attitudes? What did Jesus say in the sermon on the mount regarding this?
4. Is salvation based upon good works? If not, what then is it based upon?
5. What did Jesus mean by the parable of the sandy foundation? What happens to the personality of a man who is only a hearer and not a doer?
6. Can a man successfully live by two systems of values? Why not?
7. What are the characteristics of a well founded personality?
8. How can parents help their children develop the proper attitudes toward life?
9. Why were the multitudes astonished at the teachings of Jesus?

Chapter 13

Finders Keepers

"FINDERS KEEPERS ... losers weepers," so goes a rule of childhood behavior. The point of this childish attitude is that what is one person's loss is another's gain.

There is a lesson to be learned here. Two individuals with the same background and the same resources can be faced with an identical problem. For the one it is no problem at all, for he has the spiritual strength to overcome it. The other individual, however, is unable to meet the challenge. He is left unhappy and without purpose.

Two young people leave home and go to college. They both come from good Christian homes; each has had good Bible training in Sunday morning church school. The one individual is able to obtain a good education and remain "faithful to the church" throughout his college years. The other "loses his faith," is left miserable and brings heartache to his parents. What is the reason for this?

The Importance of Attitudes

This study of the Sermon on the Mount has shown above all that Jesus emphasized the proper attitudes. Rather than legislating, rather than providing a catalog of rules concerning moral behavior, Jesus stressed the importance of developing the right inner dispositions of heart. This was perhaps one of the reasons his teaching was authoritative, whereas that of the scribes and Pharisees was not. Jesus reached into men's hearts and provided the key to happiness.

Christianity is not a set of facts to be memorized, a creed to be recited, nor a set of rules to be accepted. It is a life to be lived and an attitude to be developed. In the day of judgment, the Lord is not going to ask each person to name the parables, the judges of Israel, the genealogy from Adam to Noah or the twelve apostles.

Rather, he is going to call into account each individual upon the basis of his relationship to Christ.

A good student carefully prepares for his final examination. Not only does he study the material which he has been given in class, he also tries to prepare for the kind of examination he will face. A student who has prepared himself to answer specific questions will be unprepared for the exam if the instructor asks for general statements about the material.

God has not left us uninformed as to the nature of our final examination. In Matthew 25:35, 36 the Lord gives an indication of what he expects: "I was hungry and you gave me food, I was thirsty and you gave me drink, I was a stranger and you welcomed me, I was naked and you clothed me, I was sick and you visited me, I was in prison and you came to me." Judgment, then, will demand the proper attitude toward God which is reflected in right attitudes toward other men.

This does not mean that salvation will be granted upon the basis of meritorious service, for the Bible makes perfectly clear that "he saved us, not because of deeds done by us in righteousness, but in virtue of his own mercy, by the washing of regeneration and renewal in the Holy Spirit which he poured out upon us richly through Jesus Christ our Savior" (Titus 3:5).

In view of the kind of final examination awaiting every person, religious education should endeavor to prepare men for it. Yet, too often Christian education becomes a process of rote memorization or sterotyped discussion. Far too many classes consist of individuals repeating things they all have heard time after time. The Bible is often treated as a book of facts, the result being that many Bible students, while able to quote vast passages from memory, never develop the important attitudes of heart stressed by Jesus and the apostles.

The Old Testament, especially, is a victim of this kind of teaching program. It is treated only as a history book. Young students are taught the historical facts of the plagues in Egypt, the Palestine invasion under Joshua, the divided kingdom and the subsequent captivity. They learn all the facts about Daniel in the lions' den and the three Hebrew children without ever developing the attitudes of heart that would enable them to resist the forces of evil the same way that Daniel, Shadrach, Meshach and Abednego did. The same youngster that grows up under this kind of teaching program goes to college and loses his faith. There must be something wrong.

The Bible is a book of history—let there be no mistake about that. But it is more than history. The Germans have a word which describes the kind of history one finds in the Old Testament —*Heilsgeschichte,* "holy history" or perhaps, "history of salvation." If a person fails to see God's redemptive activity in human history reflected in the narratives of the Old Testament, he has missed the whole point of the book. He might as well be studying the invasion of Gaul or the Peloponnesian wars.

This is not to say that facts are unimportant, for any knowledge of the Bible must be based upon the historical and cultural facts reflected in the narratives. But facts are valuable only when they serve as a skeleton for other study. The teaching of facts is useful only when the facts help convey attitudes that will transform lives.

Why So Many Losers?

The tragedy is that so many young people wind up as "losers" instead of "finders." Unsubstantiated, but frequently quoted, figures indicate that 50 percent of the young people that attend secular colleges leave the church. Are secular schools really that bad? Are the temptations faced by modern young people any worse than those faced by Daniel, Timothy, or any of the other heroes of the faith? Or, could it perhaps be that the young people who "lose their faith" never really had any faith to begin with? Perhaps they were always "losers" instead of "finders." Or, worse still, perhaps some subtle but dangerous attitudes were instilled during their formative years—attitudes that even their teachers were unaware of. Let us assume that the latter is the case, and see if we can uncover some of these attitudes.

One attitude that may be partly to blame is the "If-I-have-any-doubts-I-have-lost-my-faith" attitude. Many Christian young people have tacitly been taught that to have any doubts or misgivings is sin. How many times have you heard a teacher say, "Now before the bell rings, let's clear this up so that everybody will be straight on it." Confusion should not be left in a student's mind when this is avoidable, but students should be taught to critically examine their faith. Doubts should not be squelched. They should be brought into the open and examined.

Perhaps there is not an answer that will satisfy the student at present. Consider, for example, the problem of human suffering. rather than give a student a lot of bad answers to a difficult question just to keep him quiet, a teacher should frankly admit that this is one of the most perplexing problems anyone will ever face. A wise teacher will discuss the various possible insights into the problem, and then urge the student to trust in God in spite of not being able to understand this problem perfectly. The gates of hell tremble when a person looks around the universe, does not see any God, but still says "I believe." Satan is dealt a mortal wound when Job seeks for an answer to his suffering, finds none, but refuses to curse his God. The Christian should be willing to say, "I believe; help my unbelief" (Mark 9:24).

Too often, however, a student is chided for bringing up difficult problems that may not have pat answers. He is urged that "It is just better not to discuss that," and many teachers are noticeably uncomfortable when the discussion in class ranges beyond the scope of the printed lesson.

A student who has not been taught to be critical will have difficulties when he goes to college. Vast areas of learning will be opened up to him and he then becomes aware of many things which present problems to his faith. There is nobody around to give him pat answers to his questions; or he may become aware of problems that have no satisfactory answers at present. He has not been taught to doubt intelligently, and he is unable to handle the situation. Instead of holding on to his faith, he chucks the whole thing overboard. Another valuable soul has ended up as a "loser."

Another subtle attitude that many teachers and preachers unknowingly instill in young people is "The-opposition-is-ignorant-and-stupid" attitude. Whether it be the question of the existence of God or the use of instrumental music in worship, young people are taught that the only reason everybody does not see as we do is that they are either pigheaded or stupid, or both. A revently published tract on a doctrinal point included the pontification that those who disagree could see the error of their ways if they "will open their eyes to the facts . . ."

Many preachers openly denounce from the pulpit the study of history, psychology, philosophy, sociology, theology, and anything else they can condemn as an "ology" or an "ism." They make young people think that if they study these disciplines they will be the worse for it and their faith will be irreparably damaged. The only cure, they say, is to stay away from these doctrines of men.

Young people are done a great injustice when they are taught that all unbelievers refuse to accept Christ simply because they are ignorant. For example, we do young people a grave injustice when we teach them that anybody who does not believe in God is stupid. In the first place that is an ungodlike thing to say. In the second place, it is untrue. We would do well to admit that many well educated and intelligent people do not accept the existence of God. After all, is this not what the New Testament acknowledges when it insists that God must be accepted by faith (Hebrews 11:6)?

When young people are taught these attitudes during their formative years, they are totally unprepared to face the intellectual challenges they will face later on. The first time a young person with these attitudes meets a brilliant and well educated instructor who has no place for religion in his life, he will be forced to admit that what he had been taught from the pulpit all these years was a lie. Here is a professor who does not share his faith— but he is far from being ignorant. Faced with these facts, many young people come to feel that the stupid individual was the teacher or preacher who underestimated the opposition. Anybody who does not think that unbelief comes in fancy clothes and academic trappings is only fooling himself.

If a young person is particularly anxious to get an education, he may be overly impressed by the brilliance of an unbelieving professor and repulsed by the ignorant dogmatisms of his former teachers and preachers. He had not been taught the kind of attitudes that would enable him to meet this test, and he has soon left the church. Again, another valuable soul becomes a "loser."

Jesus never underestimated the power of Satan. He prepared for his temptations by a forty day fast in the wilderness. Young people can be prepared for the most subtle and insidious weapons of the enemy by the proper kind of religious education. This must consist of the development of the kind of inner attitudes that will enable them to withstand any temptation.

Young people must be taught the importance of the attitudes of poverty of spirit, thirst for righteousness, and fatherly love toward others. They must understand that life is more than food and clothing, and above all must be taught to trust in God even when they cannot find an answer to all their questions. They must be convinced that the Christian life is the abundant life, and that the Lord, alone, possesses the keys to happiness.

Questions

1. Why didn't Jesus offer a catalog of rules to regulate human behavior? Why did he offer guiding principles instead?

2. Why is Bible study which only emphasizes facts not an adequate program of religious education?
3. What is lacking in a purely factual study of the Bible? What teaching does this kind of study overlook?
4. What should be the characteristics of an adequate religious education program?
5. What place should the study of facts have in a properly oriented program of teaching?
6. Discuss the reason so many young people "leave the church." What are some of the reasons for this? Is it because of a lack of proper training?
7. In what ways should young people be prepared to face the doubts that will come their way? Is the attitude of questioning one's beliefs a sinful attitude?
8. Should a teacher be ashamed to admit that there may be no adequate answer to every question and problem?
9. How can a student be taught to trust in God even though he cannot understand everything perfectly?
10. How is it unfair to teach a student that the opposition is ignorant and stubborn?
11. What effect may this attitude have upon a student in later life?